# MARK

## ALEXA TEWKESBURY

## CWR

Published 2014 by CWR, Waverley Abbey House, Waverley Lane, Farnham, Surrey GU9 8EP, UK. Registered Charity No. 294387. Registered Limited Company No. 1990308.

For a list of National Distributors visit www.cwr.org.uk/distributors

Concept development, editing, design and production by CWR
Cover illustrations: Mike Henson at CWR
Internal illustrations: Ben Knight at CWR
Printed in the UK by Page Bros
ISBN: 978-1-78259-355-3

# Introduction* by Benny

There are some things you just want to know
**EVERYTHING** about. Aren't there?

Like how *really scary* monsters can look so *real* and *scary* in films.

And how aeroplanes can fly with fixed, sticky-out wings, but helicopters need whirly propellers.

And how my mate, Paul, can hold a Malteser in his mouth for *twenty minutes* without eating it! (Honestly, I'm not kidding – twenty minutes and it's not even a little bit crunched up or anything.)

And then there's Jesus. The most **AMAZING** Man who ever lived. How could anyone *not* want to know everything there is to know about Him?

I've been reading the Gospel of Mark. It's full of brilliant stories about what Jesus did while He lived on earth. Stories that show just what an incredible Teacher and Healer He is.

So that gets me thinking. If *I'd* been around in New Testament times, I'd have seen Jesus, I know I would.

I'd have gone to listen to Him.

I'd have watched Him heal people.

### I MIGHT EVEN HAVE MET HIM IN THE FLESH!

And *that* gets me thinking even more ... thinking and imagining.

If I'd been around when Jesus lived on earth, I suppose life with Topz might have been a little bit like this ...

# CHAPTER 1
## Journey Maker
### (Mark 1:35–39)

Benny runs.

Not for any particular reason. Sometimes he just runs, hurtling across the open space at the lakeside. His bare feet dig into the soft ground as they land. One, then the other. His toes flick sand into the air behind him as each leg kicks back and thrusts him forwards.

He's fast today. He skims the water's edge, sends up mini-explosions of spray. The early morning air rushes over him as he pounds through it. His skin tingles.

**'WHAT'S THE HURRY?'** calls a voice.

A fisherman sits in his boat pulled up on the beach. A large fishing net is draped over his knees. He leans over it to mend a tear.

Benny doesn't answer; doesn't really catch the words. He just lifts a hand to wave and pelts on to the far end of the lakeside.

At last he stops. He gasps for breath and his chest heaves. His heart thuds inside it as if it's trying to break free.

Hands on hips, he turns. He gazes along the length of the shore where he has just run. There's no one else in sight. Just the old fisherman bent over his net. Sometimes Benny gets up early in the morning – so early it's barely light – for exactly this: the beach almost all to himself and the freedom to run with nothing and no one in the way.

'Phew!' he whistles when he's recovered enough breath. 'Starving now.'

He starts to wander back towards the fishing village near the shores of Lake Galilee; towards Capernaum.

By now, the sun has crept up above the line of the horizon. It washes the sky in golden light. It'll be another hot day.

Up ahead of Benny, a group of men appear on the beach. They stand for a moment. Then they separate and fan out across the shore.

Benny slows. He hears one of them call out: **JESUS!**

He looks around, but there's no sign of Jesus on the beach.

Benny hears the name called again. When he glances back at the men, he thinks perhaps they must be searching for Him.

One of the men walks purposefully in his direction. He gets closer and Benny recognises one of Jesus' disciples, Simon Peter. He can't see the faces of the other men well enough, but they are probably Jesus' disciples, too.

Simon Peter doesn't speak to Benny as he passes. He looks preoccupied; almost worried, Benny thinks.

Why? Has something happened? Has something happened to Jesus?

Benny walks on. He feels a knot in the pit of his stomach. What could be wrong? Why are Jesus' friends looking for Him? Where could He be?

The streets of Capernaum that had been asleep when he went down to the lake are awake now. Groups and huddles of people wander along together or stand around. They speak in low voices. More people start to join them. They seem hesitant; unsure what to do. Waiting.

Benny catches a woman's eye. 'Have you … seen Jesus this morning?' he asks.

The woman shakes her head. 'No one has. We've all turned out to see Him, but there's no sign. Even His disciples don't know where He's gone.'

The knot in Benny's stomach tightens. This isn't right, is it? This can't be right.

He twists round and runs. Not just because he feels like running this time but because he wants to catch up with Simon Peter. He wants to help hunt for Jesus.

In no time he's back at the lakeside. He stops on the shingle; looks right and left. All the way from one end of the beach to the other. There are more fishermen now. They get ready to work, preparing their boats to go out on the lake and fish.

But he can't see any of Jesus' disciples.

Again he runs. In the direction he'd seen Simon Peter go a short while before. Out towards the open countryside. It's lonely there but he doesn't worry that he might get lost; he doesn't care. He just wants to find Simon Peter. Better still, he wants to find Jesus.

Benny slows at last and breathes heavily. He feels hot and sticky. As the sun climbs higher, the morning air isn't fresh and cool anymore.

What was that?

There's a noise somewhere over in the trees. No, not a noise – a voice!

Benny steals towards it. He hopes, **PLEASE LET IT BE PETER!**

In amongst trees, he sees a man. Then two men. One of them is Simon Peter.

Benny inches forward a little more. He needs to see better but he doesn't want to be spotted.

Another man is there, too. There's a group of them.

But what about the One they're all looking for? What about Jesus?

A twig cracks under Benny's foot. He sucks in a breath; freezes.

No one turns. No one has heard. They are too intent on their conversation.

'It's not just us,' says Simon Peter. 'Everyone is looking for You.'

That's when Benny sees Jesus. He steps forward into the clearing. He's all right! Benny was afraid He'd been hurt or wounded, but He's all right.

Jesus studies Peter's face a moment before He answers.

'Do you think this is the only place that needs me?' He asks. 'There are other villages full of people who need to hear my teaching. We can't just stay here, we must go there, too. All over the place.'

He pauses. He looks intently at His friend, Peter.

'I didn't come to stay in just one spot,' He says. 'I came to speak to as many people as I can while I'm living on the earth. I'm a journey maker, Simon Peter.'

Benny watches as Jesus steps away out of the clearing; out of sight. He would do as He said, Benny knew that. He would travel far and wide to teach people about God; to work miracles and to make people well. This was the work His Father had sent Him to do and He would do it.

Jesus' disciples look at each other. They set off after Him. In the opposite direction from Capernaum.

After they've gone, the clearing in the trees stands silent and empty.

# CHAPTER 2
## Clean
### (Mark 1:40–45)

**'HOLD ON, CAN'T YOU?'** calls Sarah. **'I CAN'T KEEP UP.'**

'Of course you can,' shouts John over his shoulder. 'You've just got to walk quicker.'

Topz follow Jesus. There's a village somewhere near. That's where He must be headed.

He is there in the distance; walking. But suddenly, as He reaches the brow of a shallow hill and makes His way down the other side, they lose sight of Him.

'It's all right for you,' Sarah moans. 'You can go as fast as you want and Gruff just follows you. But I have to carry Saucy. And I know she's only little but after a few miles she starts to weigh a ton.'

'A ton!' laughs Benny. 'Bit of an exaggeration there, Sarah.'

Sarah frowns. 'Not an exaggeration at all, *actually*. And how would you know anyway? You've never had to carry her anywhere.'

'Do you want me to take her for a bit?' asks Josie.

'I think Benny should take her,' Sarah mutters.

'Go on, then. I don't mind.' Benny stops and holds out his arms.

Sarah looks at him for a second, shaking her head. 'No, it's all right. Saucy likes to be with me when we go somewhere new. She needs to feel safe. But ... thanks.'

Benny shrugs. 'Let me know if you change your mind.' And off he goes again, half walking, half trotting to catch up with the others.

Sarah sighs and raises her eyes. 'You could slow down a bit, though,' she grumbles.

Danny reaches the top of the hill. He points. 'It's all right. We haven't lost Him. There He is.'

The other Topz cluster round. They wait a moment for Sarah to catch up.

Paul peers into the distance. 'Wait a minute. Who's that?'

There's another figure on the plain below them. Someone well-covered in wraps and shawls hurries towards Jesus.

**'SHOULD WE WARN HIM?'** says Benny. 'It might be a robber. Come on!'

Benny goes to run down the short hill slope, but Danny stops him. 'No, wait. I think it's all right.'

The figure who stops a short way away from Jesus suddenly drops to the ground to kneel in front of Him, and slowly pulls down the cloth head covering.

Jesus gazes at the man. Topz stare, shocked.

Josie whispers, 'What's wrong with him?'

'He's got some sort of skin disease,' murmurs Danny. 'Look at his face.'

'Then he shouldn't be near Jesus, should he?'
John frowns. 'That sort of disease – I've heard it's
really catching.'

Dave shakes his head. 'Jesus never sends anyone
away. You know He doesn't.'

The sick man keeps his head low. He seems ashamed.
He can't bring himself to look into Jesus' face.

But Jesus stoops to look straight into his.

'Help me, Jesus,' the man begs. His voice is choked.
Desperate. 'If You want to, Jesus, I know You can make
me clean. Please …'

Jesus watches the man, eyes brimming with sadness;
filled with pity.

He reaches out a hand and touches him.

'Of course I want to,' He says. 'You are clean now.'

At once, the man is healed. The disease is gone!
The skin on his face, his hands, his whole body, is
once again smooth and clear. Just as it was before he
became ill.

The man stares in disbelief at his fingers, at his hands.
He scrabbles at his sleeves; pulls them up to inspect the
skin on his arms.

Finally, he lifts his eyes to look at Jesus. Full in the face.

The sadness in Jesus' eyes has gone. Now they are bright with love for the man in front of Him. They dance with excitement to see him well again.

But when Jesus speaks, His voice is stern.

'Now, I need you to listen to me,' He says. 'You're not to breathe a word of this anywhere. Is that clear? You must keep quiet about what has happened to you. Just go straight to a priest and ask him to check your skin. Then thank God that He has made you better.'

Josie gazes, eyes wide. 'Jesus touched him,' she murmurs. 'He touched that man. No one else would have touched someone with a disease like that.'

Sarah hugs Saucy and nestles her cheek into the softness of her fur. 'No one else can touch someone and make them better,' she smiles.

'D'you think He was scared?' wonders Josie. 'D'you think Jesus was scared that if He touched him, He might catch it, too? If He was, just think how brave He's been. How much He must have cared that the man should get well.'

'I think Jesus wants more than for the man to be well,' Dave says. 'I think He wants him to have his life back. People with that skin disease – they have to stay away from everybody. They have to stay alone. Jesus wants him to see a priest so that the priest can tell people he's all right now. He's better. Then he'll be able to be with his family and friends again. He'll be able to go and worship God with other people in the Temple again. Because of Jesus, he won't have to be on his own anymore.'

As Topz watch, the man stumbles backwards. He still can't believe he is well. Then away he runs.

But even as Jesus continues His journey, the man He has healed can't keep the news to himself. Everywhere he goes, he tells people how sick he was – and now how well he is. Thanks to Jesus' miracle touch.

Word spreads fast as the man talks and talks. Before long, so many people are desperate for Jesus to help them that He has to stay away from the nearby towns and villages. As soon as He is spotted, He is swamped by crowds.

Instead, He spends time in quiet, lonely places, away from houses and markets and communities; the places where other people don't tend to go.

It's several days before He even makes His way home to Capernaum.

But still they find Him. Still they come to Him.

'Why doesn't Jesus want people to know what He's doing?' asks John. 'They get to know anyway because no one He helps can keep quiet – but why doesn't He want them to talk about Him?'

'He doesn't want everyone to know that He's God's Son, I suppose,' says Josie. 'Not yet.'

Dave nods his head. 'There are people who aren't going to like what Jesus says and does. Important people. People with lots of power. And Jesus has got heaps of teaching to do before He wants them to hear about everything He's doing.'

# CHAPTER 3
## Up Close
### (Mark 2:1–4)

The streets of Capernaum are alive with people.

**'JESUS IS BACK! JESUS IS HOME!'** The excited murmur chases its way all through the village.

People jostle and push, eager to get inside the house where He is teaching. To be able to see Him and hear Him up close.

Benny and Josie stand just inside the doorway.

'Where are the others?' says Josie. 'I wish they hadn't been late meeting up. They'll never get in here now.'

A man and a woman squeeze themselves into the house beside the two Topz, jamming them up against the wall. Benny tries to shift along a little, but there's just no more space.

'They'll never get in and we'll never get out,' he grunts. 'And it's boiling in here. Can you even breathe properly?'

'Just about,' grins Josie. 'Oh, well. At least if we faint, we won't fall over. There's no room to fall anywhere.'

Outside the door of the house, the crush of people is just as thick. It spills all across the street.

Minute by minute, more and more onlookers turn up and add to the crowd.

As Jesus begins to speak, the room falls quiet; people at the front shush those further back until everyone stops talking and listens. The chat and murmurs of the huge huddle outside can still be heard in the background.

Squashed up against the wall, Benny tries to concentrate. He can't see Jesus from where he is. But if he can just focus on His voice ...

Instead, his attention keeps being drawn to the voices outside the door.

'We should have got here earlier ... We'll have to catch Him when He comes out ... I just want to see Him ... At least you've met Him before ...'

Suddenly, through the buzz of chit-chat, Benny makes out another voice. Several men's voices. They sound urgent; anxious. They cut through the other conversations.

'We can't even get to the door,' says one.

'Even if we could, we'd never get in the house. It's jam-packed in there,' says another.

'Well, what are we going to do?' asks a third. 'We've come all this way to see Jesus. We can't give up now.'

'Maybe we should wait a bit,' a fourth suggests. 'These people have gotta go home sooner or later.'

'No.' The first voice again. 'No, we might miss Him if we do that. And we can't afford to miss Him.'

Benny tries to peer round the man and woman who have crammed themselves next to him in the doorway, so as to catch a glimpse of the speakers. He can't see into the street. Even if he could, he has no idea where they are in the crowd outside.

But he knows there's something very wrong. He can hear it. There are men somewhere outside the house who desperately need to see Jesus, and Jesus doesn't even seem to know they are there.

Benny glances at Josie. Perhaps she has heard the men's talk, too. She stands on tiptoe and cranes her neck to try to see over the heads of the people in front of her. It's clear all she can hear is Jesus. All she *wants* to hear is Jesus.

Benny turns his head back towards the door. The anxious voices outside have stopped.

Have the men left? Have they decided to wait until later to see Jesus after all? Once again, Benny tries to concentrate. Jesus is talking and he wants to listen. Why does he find it so hard sometimes just to listen ...?

## WHAT'S THAT?

Benny isn't the only one to have heard it.

A clunk. Then several clunks.

A few heads in the crowded room turn, look around, look at each other, then turn back to listen to Jesus.

There's another clunk. Jesus doesn't stop talking.

There's a shuffling, scraping noise.

Benny looks all around. Where's it coming from?

Even Josie can hear it now. She throws Benny a glance. He shrugs at her. The noises get louder. There are creaks and cracks.

All of a sudden, at the very front of the room – right over Jesus' head – a shower of dust falls from the ceiling.

Jesus glances up; a murmur runs through the crowd of listeners.

There's another sprinkling of dust and Jesus steps back out of the way. He looks half surprised; half curious.

Everyone's gaze turns towards the roof.

'What's going on?' Josie hisses. 'What's happening up there?'

A small hole appears in the ceiling and a shaft of sunlight trickles through it down to the floor. Dust swirls in the brightness of the beam.

'I dunno what it is,' Benny mutters. He swallows. His mouth feels dry in the stifling heat of the house. 'But there's something on the roof ... And it's trying to get in ...'

There's more cracking. Sounds of tearing.

The hole gets bigger and bigger as the roof covering is dug at; dragged at.

People look a bit scared now but no one even tries to run outside. There'd be no point. It would be impossible; they're too tightly packed into the room.

They can only stand and wait and listen and watch, along with Jesus. They can only bite their lips and stare upwards.

And wonder what on earth is trying to get in through the roof!

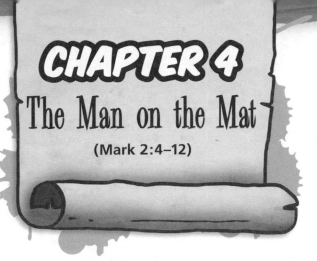

# CHAPTER 4
## The Man on the Mat
### (Mark 2:4–12)

A face appears.

A man's face.

Then another.

Then four men's faces lean over the opening that's been torn out of the roof. They gaze down at the sea of faces in the room below, which gaze up.

There's silence.

Until someone in the crowd laughs. Then someone else starts to laugh, too. There are giggles and chuckles of relief all over the room.

Benny's grin spreads across his face. He leans in towards Josie.

'Not a gigantic, roof-munching wild animal, then,' he whispers.

Josie grins back at him.

Jesus steps forward. He looks up through the hole; up at the faces that peer down.

**'I'M SORRY,'** one of the men says. **'WE REALLY HAD TO SEE YOU, JESUS. WE COULDN'T THINK OF ANY OTHER WAY.'**

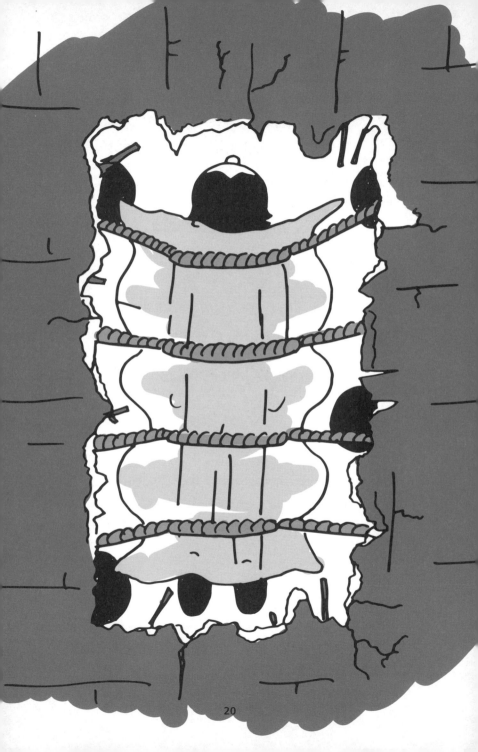

Benny recognises the voice. He knows instantly who these men are.

They are the men who were outside when Jesus began to teach. The anxious men who needed to find a way into the house to see Him.

The faces disappear. For a moment there is just the gaping **HOLE IN THE ROOF**.

Then it is filled with something; a mat tied at each of its four corners with rope. The men use the rope to lower it down. As it nears the floor, the man who lies on the mat can be clearly seen.

He doesn't speak. He looks ill. Thin. He stares upwards with wide, frightened eyes. He doesn't move because he can't.

The man on the mat is paralysed.

When the four men have lowered him safely to the floor, once again they peer down through the hole they've made.

They say nothing. They don't need to. One look at their paralysed friend and Jesus knows exactly why they are there. He can see what faith they have in Him. How firmly they believe that He will make the man on the mat better. They couldn't get into the house so they climbed all the way up to the roof and dug a hole in it. All to be able to place their friend in front of Him.

Jesus crouches down beside the man. He looks into his frightened face. He smiles.

Quietly, He says, 'It's all right. All the things you've done wrong – they're forgiven.'

There are whispers and frowns among the onlookers. They glance at each other. Some with surprise and wonder – others in disbelief.

Near the front, to one side of the room, sit some teachers; men whose teaching is completely different to Jesus'. They teach in the Temple. They teach about God. But they don't tell people about His love for them. They don't speak about His care and His forgiveness. They talk only about the Law. The rules. What you must do, what you mustn't do.

They don't try to love other people the way God wants them to.

The teachers wear disapproving looks on their faces. They have disapproving thoughts in their heads.

Suddenly, Jesus swings around. He stares at them. He knows exactly what's going on in their minds.

'You wonder about me, don't you?' He says. His voice is no longer quiet and gentle as it was when He spoke to the paralysed man. 'You wonder how I dare to speak the way I do. God is the only One who can forgive the wrong things people do, right? So how do I dare to tell this man that his sins are forgiven?'

The room is silent.

'Why do you think like that?' Jesus goes on. 'Let me ask you this. What's easier? To say to this man, "Your sins are forgiven", or to tell him to get up, roll up his mat and walk?'

The teachers say nothing. They just fix Jesus with hard, unforgiving eyes.

Jesus says, 'I will prove to you that I can forgive

sins here on earth. That I, the Son of Man, have the *authority* to forgive sins.'

He turns to the man on the mat and smiles at him.

'It's time to get up,' He says. 'Get up and pick up the mat you're lying on. Then go home.'

The man sucks in a deep breath.

In front of the whole room – in front of his four friends on the roof – slowly, carefully, he lifts his head and props himself up on his elbows. He gulps and gasps more breath into his lungs.

He pushes himself into a sitting position.

He presses down into his feet, pushes up. Until he's standing. Standing in front of Jesus on the floor.

The man can't speak to Him. He has no words to express how he feels. It's been so long since he could move that it's as much as he can do to stay upright.

He bends down and he picks up his mat. Just as Jesus has told him to do.

And then he walks.

There was no space in the room. When Jesus began to teach, people were jammed in so tightly they couldn't move.

But somehow now, they make a way through for the man on the mat.

He walks. He weaves through the onlookers and squeezes between them. He reaches the doorway. Benny and Josie stare at him. There's a glow in his cheeks. A spark in his eyes.

And with his mat under his arm, he slips out into the street.

# CHAPTER 5
## The Whole Point*
### (Mark 2:13–17)

'He walked, Sarah!' beams Josie. 'I wish you'd seen it! He was paralysed – just lying there – but when Jesus told him to, he got up and he walked!'

'I knew it. I knew something had happened!' Sarah turns to the rest of the Gang. 'I told you, didn't I? We couldn't get anywhere near the house. There were just too many people. But suddenly we could hear all the cheers and shouts.'

'*Hear* them?' Benny grins. 'Josie and me, we were deafened by them! People all over the room started praising God *really* loudly. I've never heard anything like it.'

'Because they'd never *seen* anything like Jesus' miracle,' Josie adds. 'That's what they were saying. All around us. "We've never seen anything like this!"'

'And we missed it,' grunts John. 'Typical.'

'Well, don't blame us,' shrugs Sarah. 'It was your fault.'

'No, it wasn't. It was Gruff's. He ran off down by the lake.'

Gruff looks up at John. His tongue lolls out of his mouth. His tail wags.

'I don't know what you're looking so cheerful about,' John mutters. 'We just missed something stonking because you decided to go off and hunt … octopuses.'

Danny gives him a sideways look. **'REALLY? HUNT OCTOPUSES?'**

'Well … hunt something anyway.'

'There might be octopuses in the lake,' says Dave. 'We should go and ask the fishermen.'

Sarah makes a face. 'I'm not sure I really want to know.'

'What's wrong with octopuses?' asks Benny. 'How cool would it be to have that many legs? If I had eight legs, I could run *so* fast! You'd hardly be able to see me, let alone catch up with me.'

'You don't know that,' retorts Sarah. 'Octopuses aren't built for running, are they? They're built for swimming. If you had eight legs on land, you might spend the whole time tripping over your feet because there'd be so many of them.'

Benny shakes his head. 'I don't think so. What about spiders? They're stonkingly quick.'

'Thanks,' Sarah groans. 'Now, not only am I thinking about octopuses, I am also thinking about spiders running at one hundred miles per hour.'

'Oh yeah,' nods Benny. 'One hundred miles per hour at least. Don't close your eyes, Sarah. They'll get you just like *that*.'

He snaps his fingers in front of her face.

'You're *so* not funny,' she grunts.

Paul giggles. 'Let's go back to the lake anyway,' he says. 'Gruff can finish doing whatever it was he was doing, and we can have a picnic.'

They wander off to find the lakeside heaving with people.

John stoops down, picks Gruff up and tucks him under his arm. 'Looks like octopus-hunting's off,' he says into the little dog's ear.

Sarah raises her eyes. 'Can everyone, please, just stop mentioning octopuses!'

Topz know Jesus must be on the beach somewhere. If a crowd gathers, He's always the reason.

They walk along the upper edge of the shingle, trying to catch a glimpse of Him.

'Isn't that Him there?' Danny points.

Jesus strolls along and people follow Him. He talks to them as He walks.

Topz follow, too, trying to catch what He's saying; to hear snippets of His teaching.

Before long, they find themselves in streets among buildings again. They walk on until Jesus slows then stops outside an open doorway. He looks in.

A man sits there. A tax collector in the middle of his work.

Jesus watches him a moment. Then, as if He's forgotten the mass of people with Him, He calls out: 'You're Levi, aren't you?'

The man looks up. He frowns when he sees Jesus.

**'COME AND FOLLOW ME, LEVI,'** Jesus says – and the man's frown vanishes. His eyes glow with surprise.

Topz notice people in the crowd nudge each other. They hear someone behind them whisper, 'Why's Jesus asking Levi to follow Him? I mean, of all people!'

A woman adds, 'Yeah, a *tax collector*.' She almost spits out the words. 'As dishonest as the day is long. Somebody ought to warn Jesus about people like him.'

'I think Jesus already knows,' Dave murmurs to himself. 'I think that's the whole point.'

In the house, Levi stands up.

He doesn't tidy away his work; he doesn't even give it a second glance. Instead, he fixes his eyes on Jesus and walks towards Him in the doorway.

The people clustered there fall back to let him through, watching as Jesus moves away and Levi follows after Him. Some shake their heads disapprovingly. Others seem confused.

'Who is this Man?' they ask each other. 'What's it all about?'

Benny looks the other way down the street. Back towards the lake.

'The beach'll be empty again now,' says Benny.

'Shall we go back there and have our picnic? My stomach's rumbling like a volcano.'

'I think we'd hear it if it was rumbling like a volcano, Benny,' grins Paul. 'But, yeah. Let's go back to the lake.'

The Gang turn to go. All except Dave, who still watches Jesus and Levi as they walk away.

'You coming, Dave?' asks Paul.

'Erm, yeah,' he answers vaguely. Then, 'Actually, no. You go. I'll come and find you later.'

Dave can still just about see Jesus. If he hurries, he'll catch up with Him. He wants to know what will happen now that Jesus has invited a man everyone hates to be one of His special friends; one of His disciples. After all, Levi is known as a thief and a crook. Jesus knows what He's doing but will anyone else understand?

A little later, as Jesus sits down with His other disciples in Levi's house to share a meal with him, they are joined by more tax collectors. All are dishonest men who steal from the people they're supposed to collect tax money from.

There are others around the table, too, who, for one reason or another, are disliked and distrusted; avoided where they live and work.

Dave has questions but no one to answer them. He has ideas as to why **JESUS** mixes with the people He does, but no one to tell him whether he's right.

He sees a group of men. They march purposefully down the street towards Levi's house. Dave recognises them as Pharisees. These are the religious teachers who disagree with Jesus' teaching. They don't like Jesus one bit.

At Levi's house, they stop. Some of them peer in through the window. Others at the door. Their faces are cold and hard. They shake their heads and they tut.

One of Jesus' disciples sees them and steps outside. He wonders what they can be staring at.

A Pharisee hisses at him nastily, 'This Jesus.' He tosses his head in the direction of the house. 'Why does He spend time with evil people like this? Why does He eat with them?'

It isn't the disciple who answers. It's Jesus Himself. He steps forward, away from the table.

'It isn't people who are well who need to see a doctor, is it?' Jesus says. His voice is quiet. Patient. 'A doctor is needed by people who are sick. And it's the same with me. I haven't come to spend my time with good, honest people. Why do they need my help? I've come to call and to teach the ones no one else will have anything to do with.'

Dave turns; slips away. His cheeks feel hot with excitement. He's understood something about Jesus before anyone has had to explain it to him.

And now he's heard Jesus Himself say it.

It's not the people who love and obey God already that Jesus needs to reach. It's the ones who are lost. The ones who spend their time doing wrong things and living their lives in wrong ways.

The ones who have no idea who God is.

Jesus is like a doctor for sick people.

That's the whole point.

# CHAPTER 6
## Rules that Make No Sense
### (Mark 2:23–28)

Danny, John and Josie throw themselves into cartwheels across a patch of rough ground. One after another after another. They race in cartwheels between two trees.

Danny is first to arrive at the second tree, followed by Josie, then John. They collapse on top of each other. A tangle of giggling, dizzy, breathless arms and bodies and legs.

'Who's next?' Danny calls.

'Me!' shouts Sarah. 'Paul, d'you wanna go?'

Paul looks doubtful. 'Someone'll have to hold my glasses,' he says.

'Who's going to hold Paul's glasses?' Sarah asks. 'And whoever it is, can they hold Saucy, too? If I turn my back, she might sneak off.'

'Trouble is,' frowns Paul, **'IF I'M NOT WEARING MY GLASSES, I WON'T BE ABLE TO SEE WHERE I'M GOING.'**

'No one can see where they're going when they're

doing cartwheels,' says Benny. 'Not really. That's half the fun.'

Paul doesn't look convinced. 'Is it? Glad you told me.'

'I'll hold them,' offers Dave. 'I don't mind.'

'Don't you want to do a cartwheel race?' asks Sarah.

Dave shakes his head. 'Too hot for cartwheeling. Give me Saucy.'

With Sarah's little cat cradled in his arms and Paul's glasses tucked carefully into his pocket, he leaves the others to their races and wanders off.

The countryside is peaceful, but alive with sound: the Gang's laughter, cries of birds, the rustle of crops in the cornfields as the wind chases through them.

There are voices, too. Somewhere. Not his friends' voices. These are the voices of men.

Dave holds Saucy in the crook of his arm, lifting his other hand to shade his eyes from the sunlight, and peers across the farmland.

Jesus is there. He walks through the fields. His special friends, the disciples, walk with Him. They talk. The disciples pick a few ears of corn to munch on as they go.

Another voice rings out. The peace is shattered.

**'JESUS!'**

Jesus turns. The disciples turn, too. Dave follows their gaze.

'What do You think You're doing?' The voice is harsh. Scolding. 'You can't let Your disciples do that! Picking corn on the Sabbath? That's against our Law, You must know that.'

Dave frowns.

The man who speaks is a Pharisee. The men with him are Pharisees, too. Once again, they eye Jesus. Their faces are full of mistrust. Just as they had been when Dave had seen them outside Levi's house.

Once again, they challenge Jesus because He doesn't teach what they teach. He doesn't live the way they want Him to live. Their 'Law' is strict and rigid. Their rules for life don't come from God, the way Jesus' rules do.

Jesus knows God's command that one day a week should be a day to think about Him and to talk to Him. A rest day. A day to be quiet. To spend time with family and friends.

Jesus knows about God's day – the Sabbath. Of course He does.

But He also knows why God made the Sabbath.

He swings around to face the Pharisees. He doesn't tell His disciples to stop picking corn. He doesn't say sorry to the Pharisees for breaking the 'Law'. Because that's not what He and His disciples are doing.

Instead, He says, 'You know the story of King David, don't you?'

Dave does. He has read all about him. King David is written about in the Old Testament.

The Pharisees study Scripture. They must know about King David, too.

'Haven't you ever read about the time when David and his men were hungry?' Jesus asks. 'They were so hungry that they went to a priest and asked him for some bread. The only bread the priest had was bread that had been blessed so that it could be offered to God.

'Now, the "Law" you teach says that only priests are allowed to eat this bread. But King David – he ate some of it. He shared some of it with his men, because they were hungry and they needed food.'

Jesus looks from one Pharisee to another, to another. He sees the hardness in their faces; the hate in their eyes.

'God made the Sabbath because it is a good thing for people to have a day of rest and to spend time with Him,' He says. 'He didn't make people to be trapped by Sabbath rules. Don't you see that? And I, the Son of Man,' He adds, 'am Lord of the Sabbath day.'

Jesus and His disciples wander on through the fields.

The Pharisees watch them. They scowl. They shake their heads.

And Dave walks away. He doesn't want to look at them anymore. He doesn't want to be near them.

He wants to talk to God.

*Why can't they see, God? Why don't they understand?*

*Jesus has come to teach us about who You are. About Your love. He's come to tell us that we don't have to live without You. You want to forgive us for the wrong things we do. The things that can separate us from You. You want to share our lives every day. You want us to be Your friends!*

*Life with You isn't about following rules that make no sense. It's about living the way You want us to, because that's what's best for us. Your rules are for our good. Like Jesus says, they're not there to trap us, they're to help us make the most of everything.*

*But the Pharisees' rules – they started off being Your rules, but now they just seem to be a way for the Pharisees to feel that they're in charge. That they're big and important and powerful. That they're the only ones who are right.*

*Only they're not right, are they? They're wrong.*

*Why can't they see, God? Why don't they understand?*

*Why WON'T they understand?*

In the distance, Dave hears Topz. They still shout and laugh and fall over each other as they cartwheel. But he doesn't want to join in.

The Pharisees are out to cause trouble for Jesus. Real trouble.

And he knows that's exactly what they will do.

# CHAPTER 7
## Worse than Troublemakers
### (Mark 3:1–6)

**'I'M SO HOT, I'M MELTING,'** Josie moans.

They walk through a narrow street of houses. They've left their cartwheeling racetrack behind them.

'It's worth it, though,' smiles Sarah. 'Now you know you're the official Topz cartwheeling champion of the year.'

'I'm second,' Danny points out. 'Second official Topz cartwheeling champion of the year.'

'Neither of you would have beaten me if I hadn't been so hungry,' grunts Benny. 'I don't know how you lot operate on so little food.'

Josie throws him a glance. 'Benny, we'd just had lunch.'

'I'm just glad to have my glasses on again,' shrugs Paul. 'I've been cartwheeling through a world of blobs … Blurry blobs … Which is a bit sick-making, if I'm honest.'

'Can we go to the river?' Josie puffs. 'I've got to wash off.'

Benny nods. 'Yeah, in a minute. Food first.'

They turn the corner into another, wider street.

At the end of the road is the synagogue. People cluster around the doors.

'D'you reckon Jesus is teaching in there?' Dave says. 'He was walking in the fields while you were racing. He must have got back here first.'

He looks at Josie. 'I know you're hot but can we go and listen? Just for a minute?'

Topz weave their way amongst the little group that hovers at the synagogue doorway and slip inside.

It's cool in the building, out of the sun. Josie closes her eyes and blows out her cheeks. The colder air refreshes her skin.

Jesus stands up at the front. There are people gathered around. They listen to Him. Some stand, some sit.

More Pharisees are there, too. Dave spots them instantly. A huddle of men to one side of the building. They watch Jesus closely.

And Dave watches *them*.

'What are they waiting for now?' he mutters.

'Who?' asks Benny.

'Them.' Dave nods his head towards the Pharisees.

'Troublemakers,' whispers Benny. 'They're hanging around Jesus more and more.'

Jesus' eyes flick towards a man who sits among His listeners. He beckons to him.

'Would you come out here for a moment?' Jesus says. 'Up to the front with me.'

The man looks unsure. He glances around. Perhaps Jesus isn't even speaking to him.

But the woman next to him smiles and nods and he knows that, yes, He is.

The man pushes himself to his feet with one hand. The other hand he holds down at his side. It doesn't look real somehow. The fingers appear stiff and fixed in their awkward position.

And Topz realise why.

The man's hand is paralysed.

He shuffles forward. He looks self-conscious; uncomfortable. All eyes are on him as he stands in front of Jesus, head down.

All eyes except those of the Pharisees. They look only at Jesus. What will He do?

Jesus gives the man a smile. Then He turns to the Pharisees and speaks to them.

'What are we allowed to do on the Sabbath day?' He asks. 'What does our Law say that we can do?'

Everyone in the synagogue stares. The Pharisees don't answer.

'Well?' Jesus continues, 'Are we to help others, or to hurt them? Should we save someone's life, or take it away?'

Still the Pharisees gaze back at Him in silence.

Dave sees the glint of anger flash into Jesus' eyes; the deep sadness cross His face. These men who are dead set against Him – who hate Him and distrust Him – they are so stubborn; the way they think is so wrong.

And Jesus can't help feeling sorry for them.

He looks back at the man with the paralysed hand.

He says to him, 'I want you to stretch your hand out.'

The onlookers nudge each other. Dave's skin tingles as a whisper of excitement rustles around the building. The Pharisees stare with unkind eyes and stern faces.

Without looking at Jesus, slowly, hesitantly, the man raises his arm; stretches out his hand.

A hush falls all over the synagogue. No one even blinks. And in that one expectant moment, the hand is healed.

The man sucks in a breath. Instantly he can feel something where he's been able to feel nothing. His fingers begin to glow warm. It's as if they've been dead and are coming back to life!

He wiggles them, scrunches them into a fist, uncurls them again; stares down at them as though he is seeing them for the first time.

And the people in the synagogue gasp and cheer and laugh out loud in wonder.

Topz beam all over their faces.

Amid the noise and excitement, the Pharisees leave. They shove their way between the cheering, delighted people. They scowl; their mouths set into hard, straight lines. They push out through the synagogue doors.

'Definitely troublemakers,' says Benny.

Dave shakes his head. 'No. Worse than troublemakers.'

Jesus has just healed someone. He's shown that He can use God's power. He's defied the Pharisees by working a miracle on the Sabbath day. He's shown them up in front of a synagogue full of people.

That's not something they'll forget or forgive.

# CHAPTER 8

## Carpenter Boy

**(Mark 3:7–10)**

A boy sits cross-legged on the ground. People bustle past, barely noticing him. Even though their feet land so close and their robes almost brush his knees.

He doesn't seem bothered; just tucks into some fresh bread that rests on a wooden plate in a basket beside him. The sky overhead glares with sunshine.

### 'HEY, ISAAC!'

Isaac glances at the feet that have stopped next to him. He is about to squint up to see whose they are when a dog appears. Its tail wags cheerfully. It seems very pleased to see him.

A grin spreads across Isaac's face. 'Hello, Gruff.' He reaches out to ruffle his ears.

John, the owner of the feet, grins, too. The rest of the Gang cluster round.

'Haven't seen you for ages,' says John. 'Where have you been?'

Isaac shrugs. 'Just round and about. I've been following Jesus.' He holds up the wooden plate. 'Would you like some bread?'

A passer-by knocks into Sarah and hurries away.
Sarah looks irritated; hugs Saucy a little tighter.

'Everyone's in such a rush,' she says.

'Everyone's always in a rush when they're trying to catch up with Jesus,' Isaac answers.

'What are you doing sitting down there?' asks Benny. 'You could get trampled.'

'I was hungry. Got up early, didn't have breakfast. Besides, I do a lot of sitting in crowds these days. Never been trampled yet.'

'I'll have some bread if there's some going.' Benny plonks himself on the ground beside Isaac.

The other Topz join them.

'Makes sense to stick together,' says Paul. 'The more of us there are, the less likely we are to get trampled.'

Danny frowns. 'How d'you work that out?'

'Well, I haven't worked it out *exactly*,' Paul answers. 'I reckon I could though. With a bit of maths. A bit of probability.' He brightens. 'Would you like me to?'

'Erm, not really, no,' says Danny. 'But, thanks.'

'What's probability?' asks Isaac.

'Don't even ask,' says Josie. 'It's just something mathsy. You don't want to know.'

Isaac looks confused. **'DON'T I?'**

'Trust me,' Josie says.

Isaac glances up at the people who still stream past.

'They've come from everywhere,' he says. 'All over the place. I was talking to some of them. There's people here from Galilee, but from much further away, too.

From Judea and Jerusalem. From the east side of the River Jordan. There's even city people here from around Tyre and Sidon.'

Dave gives a half smile. 'Not much point Jesus asking people to keep quiet about Him now, then.'

'Nah!' chuckles Isaac. 'Everyone's heard. Or they will do very soon. **JESUS IS FAMOUS**.'

'He's more than famous,' Dave says.

Sarah points to Isaac's wooden plate. 'I love that.'

'Do you?' smiles Isaac. 'I made it.'

'You didn't!'

'I did! It's what I'm going to be. A carpenter. I'll work with my dad on the farm, too, like I do now. But what I really want to learn to be is a carpenter.'

Sarah peers at the plate more closely. 'You're good already, Isaac. If I tried to make a plate out of wood, it'd look like ... well, I don't know, but definitely not like a plate.'

'A sock?' suggests Benny.

Sarah raises her eyebrows at him. 'Since when have socks been made out of wood?'

'I didn't say you'd have *made* a sock,' Benny says. 'I said your plate might have *looked* like a sock. I was trying to be helpful.'

'So, Isaac,' says Josie, 'why do you want to be a carpenter?'

'Because Jesus was a carpenter,' Isaac replies. 'I reckon He still makes things, too. And I want to be like Jesus.'

Isaac packs the empty plate back into the basket. He gets to his feet and Topz follow.

They join the flow of people as it heads towards the lake.

When they arrive at the beach, it's almost impossible to move. The crowds are packed so closely together.

Jesus has already healed lots of sick people there. More and more arrive at the lakeside all the time. They press forward to reach Him, push their way through, stretch out their arms, just to try to touch Him. They know that He can make them better if they can only get close enough.

Then, from somewhere near the water, Topz hear a cry: 'He's leaving! Jesus is leaving!'

People further back start to wail. 'No! Not yet! He can't leave yet – we haven't even seen Him!'

'He's getting in a boat!' another person shouts. 'His friends have got a boat ready for Him and He's going out on the lake.'

The Gang can feel the movement in the crowd. The urgent pushing; onlookers, people who are sick or disabled, all trying to catch just a glimpse of Jesus, the Healer. Jesus, the Teacher.

'It's no wonder He's headed for the water,' someone else says. 'These crowds! There's too many people here. Way too many. He must be afraid He'll be crushed. I know I would be if I were Him. I'm not too comfortable as it is, and it's not me they've come to see!'

Gruff jumps up and rests his paws on John's hip.

'What's the matter, Gruff?' asks John. 'Too many people for you, too?'

Isaac smiles. 'Let's go back to my house. I can show you how to make a plate out of wood.'

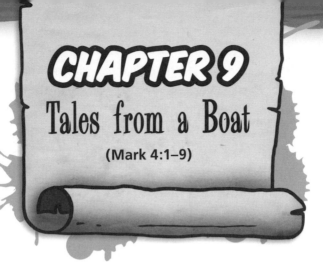

# CHAPTER 9
## Tales from a Boat
**(Mark 4:1–9)**

Josie looks up from the giant letter 'J' she is drawing in the sand.

'The beach must be one of Jesus' favourite places to be,' she says. 'He's here again.' She nods towards the Figure that strolls along by the water's edge.

A group of men walk with Him.

Sarah gazes past Jesus to the straggles of people who have begun to appear along the shore. 'Look out,' she says. 'Crowds are coming.'

She glances round for Saucy; spots her sitting on an upturned boat, and scampers over to scoop her up.

'At least we're here first today,' says Benny.

Josie puts her hands on her hips; she looks disappointed.

'They're going to trample all over my letter "J",' she grumbles. 'And I haven't even finished it yet.'

'Let's finish it now,' says Sarah. **'COME ON, REALLY QUICK.'**

'But you're holding Saucy. You haven't got your hands free.'

Sarah kicks a foot into the air. 'Got my bare toes, though,' she grins.

They decorate the huge 'J' with swirls and squiggles and stars. Sarah finds drawing with her toes trickier than she thought she would. Her stars look a little wonky.

When she and Josie have finished, the Topz boys jump, barefoot, all the way around the picture, framing it with a pattern of feet.

'Looks so good!' Josie beams.

'Yeah!' chuckles Danny. 'Work of art. Too good for anyone to walk over.'

People gather and Jesus begins to teach them. Topz stand close to the disciples. For once they have a place down at the front of the growing crowd.

But as usual when word gets out that Jesus is around, before long there are too many onlookers. Far too many come to see; to listen. There isn't enough space. They cram themselves onto the sand; onto the shingle. They shuffle between the fishing boats. They perch on rocky outcrops. The **CLOSER** they can get to Jesus the better.

And if they can't get close, they jostle and push against each other; they stand on their toes and crane their necks to glimpse just a hair on Jesus' head.

Finally, once again, Jesus has to escape out onto the lake in a boat. It's not safe to stay where He is. People wouldn't mean to hurt Him. But with so many of them pressing in on Him, He could easily be crushed.

For the second time that day, Josie's face falls with disappointment.

'Typical,' she moans. 'We've got a brilliant spot near Jesus and now He's leaving.'

'No, wait,' says John. 'I don't think He's going anywhere. I think He's just got into the boat because it's safer.'

Topz keep their eyes on Him. This time Jesus doesn't sail away across the water. He puts some space between Himself and the crowds. But John's right. He stays close enough to the shore to be seen and heard.

For a moment or two, He says nothing; just gazes at the huge numbers of people who strain to see Him, spread all across the beach.

## THEN HE STARTS TO TELL THEM A STORY.

'Listen to this!' Jesus says. 'There was once a farmer who went out into his fields to sow some corn. But as he sprinkled the seeds on the ground, some of them fell outside the fields onto the path. As soon as the birds saw it, they swooped down and gobbled it up.'

There are murmurs in the crowd: 'What's He doing? … Isn't He going to teach us about God? … Doesn't He know there are sick people here? They need Him to make them better, they don't want to listen to stories …'

Others in the crowd answer: 'Just listen! Jesus is teaching us … Sometimes He teaches by telling stories … You must be quiet and listen!'

'Some of the seeds the farmer scattered,' Jesus continues, 'they fell on ground that was very rocky, where there wasn't much soil. Because the earth there wasn't very deep, the seeds quickly sprouted little shoots.

'But then, up came the sun. It burnt the new shoots

with its heat. And because there wasn't enough soil for them to grow deep roots, they soon shrivelled up.

'There were other seeds that fell in amongst brambles,' Jesus says. 'Only, it wasn't a good place for them to be. The seeds sprouted, but as they grew, so did the brambles. Until the thorny bramble bushes were too strong for them. They choked the young corn plants.'

Once again, some in the crowd whisper to each other: 'So what happens to the farmer's crop? Does none of the seed grow?'

And once again they are answered: 'Sssh! Listen for the end of the story!'

'But there were some seeds,' Jesus smiles, 'that fell in the good, deep soil of the fields. Up sprang the shoots; taller and taller; stronger and stronger. And they produced corn. There were thirty grains on some plants. Sixty on others and one hundred on others!'

Jesus pauses to gaze along the shores of the lake. Everywhere He looks, there are eager eyes; attentive faces.

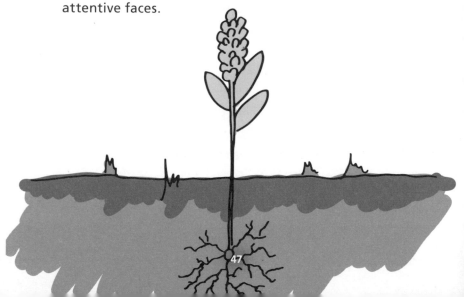

'Listen, all of you!' He calls out. **'IF YOU HAVE EARS, THEN LISTEN TO ME!'**

The story is finished.

'Did you get it?' Sarah whispers. 'I listened, but I don't know if I got it.'

'I know what you mean,' says Paul.

People behind Topz talk, too: 'I don't understand … Did you understand? … Perhaps we missed something … What have seeds got to do with God?'

Topz wait. There must be more. Jesus must be going to say something more.

But He doesn't.

And at last the crowds begin to shuffle their way off the beach at the lakeside; still with their questions, still with their wonderings.

Benny shakes his head. 'I want to know. That story means something important otherwise Jesus wouldn't have told it. I want to know what it is.'

Other voices around them say the same thing.

'Let's go back,' someone suggests. 'When it's quieter and Jesus has got a bit more space – let's go back and ask Him to explain.'

Topz glance at each other.

'Great idea,' says John. 'Why didn't we think of that?'

Little by little, the beach empties. The sand and shingle are full of dips and bumps, stirred up by so many feet.

And Josie's letter 'J' has vanished under the trampling without a trace.

# CHAPTER 10
## Searchers
### (Mark 4:10,13–20)

Late in the afternoon, Topz find Jesus again.

They search for Him with people from the morning's crowd; people who want to understand Jesus' story as much as they do. They wander through streets; comb the lakeside; hunt the hills.

Suddenly – 'There's Peter!' Dave points.

Up ahead of them is Jesus' friend. He strolls along with the other eleven disciples.

Topz and the people with them follow at a distance. Perhaps they're looking for Jesus, too.

When they spot Him, He is alone.

**'JESUS!'**

Jesus raises His head and looks towards the group of searchers.

'Jesus ...' One of them starts to speak. 'Jesus,' he says again. 'We were there. We were at the lakeside earlier. You told a story from the boat. A parable. We want to know more.'

The speaker stops and glances round at his companions.

'We didn't understand, You see. Please explain it to us.

We want to understand Your story.'

Jesus watches the man, thoughtfully.

'You didn't understand my story?' He says. 'Then I wonder how you will understand any of my stories.'

His eyes dart from one person to another.

'Listen, then,' He continues. 'The farmer who sows the seed is like someone who spreads God's message, who tells people all about God and how to live the way He wants them to.

'Now, some people are like the seeds that fell on the path. For one reason or another, they don't care about God's message. It doesn't even begin to sink in. It's forgotten as soon as it's heard; snatched away, just as the birds snatch the seed from the path.

'And remember the seeds that fell on the rocky ground?' Jesus asks. 'Some people are like that, too. They're so happy when they first hear God's message. And it does start to sink in! But the trouble is, it doesn't sink in deeply enough.

'Sadly, those people don't last long as God's friends. At the first sign of trouble, or if anyone starts to poke fun or is nasty because of what they believe, they're off! They give up on their friendship with God.'

Paul leans in to Danny.

'I never want to do that,' he whispers. 'I never want to give up on being God's friend.'

Danny smiles and nods. 'Me neither. I mean, I mess up. Loads. And sometimes I can't be bothered – going to church, reading my Bible. Talking to God, even.

But I've got to stick with it, I've just got to. I can't imagine not having God right beside me. Not ever.'

Jesus says, 'What about the seeds that fell into the brambles? They are like people, too. People who hear about God – how much He loves them and wants to forgive them for the wrong things they do. But then they let themselves get swamped with worries.

'Or they spend too much time wanting things. They chase money. They think about what they haven't got all the time, instead of being grateful for what they have. Until in the end, being friends with God isn't nearly as important as everything else is to them. Just like the brambles choke the corn plants, so their friendship with God is choked and doesn't grow.'

'*I* worry,' Sarah mumbles to Josie. 'About all sorts of things. School and friends. I worry a lot about Saucy, I can't seem to help it. But I'm still God's friend, aren't I?'

Josie smiles. 'Of course you are! God knows we find it hard not to worry. Just like He knows we find it hard not to get cross or to be mean to each other sometimes. But He wants to help. And every time you ask for His help, Sarah – and every time you *trust* Him to help you – that makes your friendship with Him get stronger and stronger.'

Sarah nods. 'I suppose I do ask for His help a lot.'

'So do I. And that's all good. Because God just wants to be involved. In everything. The good bits and the bad bits.'

Jesus says, 'But how does the story end? Some of the farmer's seed fell in the good soil, didn't it? And that's where it sprouted properly. The roots pushed deep down into the earth. The plants grew up tall and strong. They produced corn, and lots of it.

'So what is that seed like?'

No one answers. The only voice anyone wants to hear right now is Jesus' voice.

'It's simple,' Jesus smiles. 'That seed is like people who hear God's message and want to be friends with Him. They want to live His way and to do the things He wants them to do. They bear fruit like the corn plants produce corn.

'In other words,' Jesus says, '**THEY START TO GROW** into the sort of people God always meant them to be.'

Sarah nudges Josie. 'I think God means us to be the sort of people who want to learn and discover as much as we can about Him. That's why Jesus says, "Listen!" He's got so much to say about God that He wants us to hear.

'God wants us to search Him out, Josie. I want to be a searcher.'

# CHAPTER 11
## The Hand that Touches the Cloak

**(Mark 5:21–35)**

Someone pushes through a crowd at the lakeside. Heads turn as he shoves his way across the beach. A woman bumps into Danny when she tries to move out of his path.

'I'm so sorry,' she mutters. 'Didn't mean to knock into you.' She shakes her head. 'Not my fault, though. I mean, did you see that? The way that man just rammed his way right past me? And him, an official at the synagogue! Jairus his name is. He should know better.'

'Don't worry about it,' says Danny. 'He's obviously in a hurry.'

'Thinks he can just barge his way to the front to see Jesus, more like it. Well, we all want to see Him, don't we, but we don't go pushing other people out of the way to do it!'

Danny only half listens. He's caught a good look at the man's face as he makes his way past. He seems preoccupied and serious; determined somehow.

But it's his eyes that Danny notices the most.

They are full of fear.

Slowly, Danny eases himself out of the little knot of people that surround him. He takes special care not to knock into the angry woman who's just been talking to him. If he can just make his way along the edge of the crowd, he might be able to spot Jairus again and find out what the problem is.

'Jesus!'

Danny hears the man shout.

There are people perched on a rock in front of him, and there's just enough space for Danny to hop up onto it beside them.

His eyes flick to and fro over the heads of the crowd. He spots Jesus almost at once. He's hard to miss ... But where's Jairus? ... *Where's Jairus?* ... There! There he is!

The group around Jesus drops back slightly to make room for the man from the synagogue. Perhaps the people had heard him call Jesus' name, like Danny had.

And in the space they make, Jairus falls on his knees.

'My daughter, Jesus,' he gasps. 'My little girl, she is so ill. Please, please, I'm begging You – please come home with me. If You could just place Your hands on her, then I know she will get better. I know she will live.'

Jesus doesn't ask any questions. He simply nods at Jairus and tries to leave the beach with him.

But there's so little space to walk.

People start to follow. They press in on all sides.

Jairus looks tense; agitated. He wants Jesus to hurry, but hurrying is impossible. All the while, his daughter could be dying, and the two of them are stuck in a crowd with no easy way through.

From the rock, Danny watches. He fidgets. He wants to go with them; to know what will happen, to see what Jesus will do.

But if he gets down from his viewpoint now, he'll lose sight of them.

Suddenly – *who's that*?

Danny notices someone else.

Someone else who, like Jairus, stands out from the rest of the crowd.

It's a woman. Her face has the same anxious, determined look about it. As she pushes near to Jesus, she lowers her head. As if she doesn't want to be noticed.

And then Danny sees it! That one quick movement. The woman reaches out a hand and touches Jesus' cloak.

Instantly Jesus stops still, and then turns around.

Jairus doesn't notice. He keeps on pressing forward; only looks back when he hears Jesus' voice.

'Who touched me?' Jesus asks. 'Just now.'

No one answers. Onlookers glance around at each other.

'Someone touched my clothes,' Jesus says. 'I know because I could feel power go out of me. Who was it?'

Again, no one says a word.

One of His disciples leans in towards Him. 'There are people everywhere. They're crowding all around You. Why do You want to know who touched You? It could have been any of them.'

Jesus takes no notice. He keeps peering around into the faces of those closest to Him.

Danny stares. The woman is still there. Right there! Is he the only one to have seen what she did?

Slowly – very slowly – she raises her head and takes a step forward. She trembles. Danny can't see into her eyes but he knows she's frightened.

Just like Jairus, as people fall back to make some room for her, she drops to her knees in front of Jesus.

She tells Him that she's been ill for the last twelve years. Lots of doctors had treated her. She'd spent all her money on paying for them.

But they hadn't made her better. Instead, she'd got worse. And worse.

'Then I heard about You, Jesus,' she says. 'And I thought if I could just get close enough to You – if I could just touch Your clothes – then I would get better.'

She lifts her eyes to meet His. She knows, as she gazes at Him, that something inside her feels different. That she is already well again.

Jesus smiles. He speaks to her in a soft voice. A gentle voice: '**YOUR TRUST IN ME HAS MADE YOU BETTER**. Now go. Be happy. You're healed.'

The woman stands up. She turns to leave.

And, again, Danny sees her face. But not just Danny this time. Lots of people watch her, nudge each other and whisper at the miracle.

The woman isn't anxious anymore. Now she glows with health. A smile dances around her mouth. Her eyes laugh.

At that same moment, as she bustles through the crowd on her way home, there's another movement among the onlookers at the beach.

Some men push through towards Jairus; messengers who have come from his house.

Jairus looks at them; stares hard at them. He knows their news even before they give it to him.

'Your daughter, sir,' one of them says. 'We're so sorry. There's no need for you to bother Jesus now ... She's gone ... She's died.'

Jairus blinks once.

And his face turns grey.

# CHAPTER 12

## Wide Awake

**(Mark 5:36–43)**

The people clustered around Jesus fall silent.

What will He say? What will He do? He's too late.

Jairus, from the synagogue, came to Him for help. And He's too late.

Jairus stares at Jesus. He says nothing. Tears well up in his eyes. His face looks covered in shadow.

As Danny watches him, he feels tears prick at the back of his own eyes.

Jesus takes no notice of the messengers; He doesn't even look at them. He focuses his attention on Jairus.

'It's all right,' Jesus says to him. He is calm; unruffled. 'Don't be frightened, Jairus. Just believe.'

Jesus motions with a hand for Jairus to take Him to his home.

As soon as the two of them start to walk, the people gathered around try to follow.

But Jesus stops them. **'NO!'**

It's a command. There's no arguing with it.

Jesus points towards His disciples.

'Just you three,' He says. 'Peter, James and John. Just you three come with me.'

The men group together and push through the gaping, murmuring huddles of onlookers, ignoring the stares, the questions.

They push on to Jairus' house.

Up on the rock, Danny's mind races.

Can he follow? *Should* he follow? Something astonishing is about to happen, he's sure of it. How could he *not follow*?

He jumps down onto the shingle of the lakeside and edges along the fringes of the crowd. He can't see Jesus. He can't see Jairus. **HE CAN'T SEE ANY OF THEM!**

People start to break away; to wander back to their homes. Jesus has gone. Why hang around? They'll hear news of the little girl soon enough. Anyway, if she's died, what news will there be?

Danny dodges between the gaps they leave.

### 'DANNY, OVER HERE!'

He turns sharply and spots Benny, who jumps up and down beside John, waving his arms.

Then Benny points – and Danny realises he knows exactly where Jesus is.

Benny can see Him.

Danny speeds up.

'Come on, let's go,' Benny says.

'How long have you been here?'

'A while. We've been looking for you. Hurry up, we don't want to lose them.'

The Topz boys follow the five men. Gruff trots along at John's heels. There are other walkers around, too. Some step out briskly, others stroll. Topz have no idea whether they are following after Jesus. They just keep their heads down. They feel sad, so sad that a girl has died – at the same time they're full of expectation for what Jesus might do.

The beach is a way behind them now. They walk between houses; across a market place with lines of stalls set up with goods to sell. They almost lose sight of Jesus when Jairus leads Him and His disciples through a maze of narrow streets.

At last, they see Jairus stop.

There are people in the road ahead. They huddle in front of a house – Jairus' house. They sob and wail. Topz can hear them from where they stand at the far end of the street. John bends down to pick up Gruff. More than ever right now he needs his dog to stay close.

These are heartbroken people.

When they see Jairus, they look up. They say nothing, too upset to speak. They move aside from the doorway of the house to allow him to enter.

Jesus, the disciples Peter, James and John step in with him.

Inside the house, people cry, too. Jairus' wife, the little girl's mother, sits on a stool. Tears streak her face. She stares straight ahead but her eyes see nothing.

Topz move closer; stand with the people grouped near the doorway.

And Jesus speaks.

'What's the matter?' He asks. 'Why all the tears? The child hasn't died. She is asleep, that's all.'

The people gaze at Him as if He is mad. They start to laugh.

Jesus watches them a moment, then, still calm, he tells everyone to wait outside the house. All except Jairus and his wife, and His three friends. The people do as He says. They leave; shuffle out, whispering and sneaking little glances at the 'madman'. They wait in the street outside the door.

When they've gone, Jesus steps into the girl's bedroom. He beckons her parents and His friends to step inside with Him.

The girl lies on her bed. The room is dim and silent and still.

Jesus moves straight to her. He picks up her hand.

He says, 'Time to get up, little girl.'

In that same second, the girl opens her eyes.

She takes in a breath; presses her lips together, wide awake. Her glance darts from face to face in the room. She sees strangers first. Then her mother, her father.

And she smiles.

The girl's mother gasps; her hands fly to her mouth.

Jairus' eyes once again brim with tears.

The girl sits up, then gets off the bed. She steps towards her parents. They fold her up in their arms.

Jesus' disciples, who know Him so well, who have seen Him work so many miracles – Peter, James and John – they have never seen Him do anything like this.

They stand and gape. Too amazed to speak.

'Your daughter will be hungry,' Jesus says to Jairus and his wife. 'Give her something to eat. And don't tell anyone what has happened here.'

Jesus leaves them together in the girl's room, walks through the house and out of the door.

His three disciples follow Him.

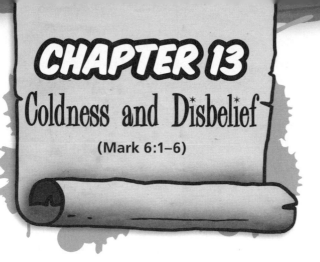

# CHAPTER 13
## Coldness and Disbelief
### (Mark 6:1–6)

They run.

Danny, John and Benny.

They stretch out their arms, feeling the rush of breeze through their hair, against their skin. The sun's heat washes over them. Their shadows ripple across the ground with them; strange and stretched, following every tiny movement.

Gruff runs, too. Across the fields, bounding, leaping, close to John's heels.

They want to feel alive; to breathe, to soak in the life God has given them.

They want to feel their hearts pound, their lungs gasp.

They want to grab hold of the world around them with every single sense in their bodies!

'She's alive!' Benny yells at the top of his voice. 'Jesus made her alive again!'

The joy and excitement inside Jairus' house had flooded out onto the street. The heartbroken people were given the news: 'Our daughter is well. Come in! **COME AND SEE, SHE'S WIDE AWAKE!'**

And the Topz boys and Gruff had started to run. Through the streets, out of the town into the countryside. They didn't stop to catch their breath.

They don't stop now.

Until the last field. It slopes gently downwards. They hurl themselves onto the ground. They laugh, they roll, they kick their legs.

They collapse flat out; lie there sucking in breath so hard and fast they think their lungs may burst.

'How do we tell the others?' It's the first thing John says when at last he is able to speak. 'They'll never believe it. You'll have to tell Sarah. One of you will. She'll never take it from me. She'll think I'm having her on. You know what she's like.'

Danny shakes his head. 'She will believe it. They all will. We know what Jesus can do, all of us. It's just actually being there when He does it – it kind of takes your breath away.'

Gruff trots ahead of them as they walk the rest of the way back to the lake. Back to find the Gang …

Jesus is walking, too. With all twelve of His disciples.

He makes a journey to His hometown now. The place where He was a child; where He learnt to be a carpenter.

Nazareth. The town where He grew up.

'How long will it take to get there?' Paul wonders. 'If we go, too, how long will it take?'

Dave shrugs. 'As long as it does, I suppose. But I wanna go.'

Topz all want to go. They want to stay close to Jesus. However much they have to walk. However long it takes.

'Besides,' says Benny, still buzzing over Jairus and the miracle girl, 'we've never been to Nazareth before. I want to see it.'

'I wonder if the people who live there now know He's on His way,' says Josie. 'They're going to be so excited!'

Sarah's eyes gleam. 'Imagine living there! Imagine the town where you live being the place where Jesus was a child!'

It's the Sabbath day when Jesus begins to teach people in Nazareth. He speaks to them in the synagogue.

Topz stand near the back. They listen. They wait eagerly to see the amazement in people's faces; to hear them murmur with wonder at Jesus' words and teaching.

They wait.

But there isn't the kind of amazement they expect. People do raise their eyebrows but there's no welcome for Jesus here. No warmth.

Just coldness. Coldness and disbelief.

'Where does He get all this stuff from?' people whisper. 'How does He talk like this? And these miracles? What's it all about, how does He do it?'

Others eye Him suspiciously. 'He's just a carpenter, isn't He? He's Mary's Son. And James, Joseph, Simon and Judas are His brothers. And don't His sisters live here?'

The questions go on. One after another.

Questions full of doubt and mistrust.

The people of Nazareth scoff at Jesus. They refuse to accept Him. They turn their backs on Him.

Topz can't believe their ears.

'What's wrong with these people?' Sarah mutters. 'How can they stand there and listen to Jesus and not believe in Him?'

Danny's heart sinks. His excitement has gone. He feels deflated; gloomy.

'Maybe because this is where He came from,' he grunts. 'Maybe it's harder for them to believe in Him because they knew Him before He started teaching. They know His family. If they knew Him when He was a carpenter, maybe they just can't accept what He's doing now.'

Jesus knows what the people of Nazareth are thinking. He can hear what they say.

Before He leaves the synagogue, He speaks to them: 'Do you know that prophets, messengers from God, are trusted and respected everywhere, except for one place. In their own hometown.

'In their hometown, no one wants to know them. Not their friends, nor their family.'

The listeners drift away.

A few sick people stay behind, but that's all. Jesus touches them and makes them better, but there is no excitement. No sense of wonder. Not really anything.

And He is sad. Sad and surprised.

He has travelled all the way to this town He knows so well. The town where He should have been greeted and welcomed.

And all he finds there is unbelief.

# CHAPTER 14
## Josie's Arrows

Paul scratches in the ground with a stick.

Josie watches him. 'What are you doing?'

'I'm ... drawing a map,' he mumbles. He concentrates; doesn't really want to talk.

'A map?' John raises his eyebrows. 'A map of what?'

'A map,' says Paul, 'of all the places Jesus has been where He's done amazing things and made people *really* happy.'

'Uh – why?' asks Danny.

'Because then we'll be able to see where Jesus has made a difference. And then we'll feel better again.'

'I don't think a map's going to make me feel better,' says Danny. 'Those people in Nazareth, they just didn't wanna know. How's a map going to help that?'

Paul sighs and carries on drawing.

'How can you draw a map anyway?' asks Benny. 'Don't you need something like a compass? And some sort of idea where all the different places are?'

Paul glances at him. 'It doesn't have to be accurate, does it? It'll just be ... rough.'

Benny looks at Paul's squiggles in the dust. 'So what's that?' He points.

'That,' answers Paul, 'is the lake. See, look. I've written "lake".'

'Oh, is that what that says,' nods Benny. **'I THOUGHT IT SAID "CAKE".'**

Paul raises his eyes. 'You'd reckon everything says "cake". Don't you ever think about anything but food? Anyway, how is that a "c"? That "l" is nothing like a "c".'

Benny tilts his head; looks at the word again. 'It is a bit. It's sort of ... well ... curvy.'

Paul narrows his eyes. He leans over, scrubs the letter out with his fist and rewrites it. Perfectly straight.

He glances at Benny. 'Better?'

'Yeah,' Benny grins. 'Except now I fancy a piece of cake.'

Paul gets back to his mapping.

'Can you remember all the names?' Dave asks.

'What names?' Paul answers.

'You know – the names of all the places.'

'Well, there's Capernaum, which I reckon is somewhere around here.' He jabs the stick into the ground; scribbles with it to make a circle. 'And then there's that place over the other side of the lake. I think it's called Gerasa. But we've not been there so I don't know exactly. And I don't know how big it is. So I'll just write "GERASA".'

He does. In capital letters along the far side of his lake. Then he scratches "CAPERNAUM" in capitals next to his circle.

'And let's face it,' Paul says, 'absolutely loads of good

stuff has happened at the lakeside. So I'm going to call that ...' He thinks a moment and sucks the end of the stick. 'I'm going to call that ... **"MIRACLE BEACH".'** He writes as he speaks.

Sarah's face lights up. 'I *love* that!' she says. 'Miracle Beach. It's perfect!'

'You see?' grins Paul. 'I knew it. This map's making us feel better already.'

Danny gives a half smile. 'It's a good map. You're doing a good thing, Paul.'

Paul studies his dusty scribbles. 'It's not really finished yet. I mean, there's lots of other places, aren't there? Only, Dave's right. I can't remember what they're all called.'

'I know what we should do,' says Josie. 'We should draw arrows.'

'Arrows?' Paul frowns.

'Can I borrow your stick?'

Paul hands it to her and she marks arrows in the dust. Long arrows beginning at the lake and spreading outwards. Some are straight; some curve. Some wiggle between the others to stretch away even further.

'Very pretty.' Paul blinks down at the map. 'Really, Josie, very ... erm ... arty. Only ... I don't quite get it ...'

Sarah's eyes trace the pattern of arrows. From their starting points, along the flow of the shafts, to the arrowheads that Josie's drawn at the tips.

'I think I do,' she says. 'I think I get it.'

John raises his eyes. 'Well, there's a surprise. Topz girls think alike, I suppose.'

'Of course we do,' answers Sarah. 'I think the

arrows show the way God's message is going to spread. It's started already, hasn't it? With Jesus being here, teaching people. They get excited about what He says and does and they talk about it. Well, not in Nazareth maybe, but everywhere else. And then *more* people get to hear. And *more* people want to know.'

'Yup,' Josie smiles. 'Topz girls think alike.'

'So do "great minds",' nods Paul. 'They think alike, too. You must both have great minds.'

John makes a face. 'I wouldn't go that far!'

Sarah ignores him. 'So that's why it doesn't matter if your map doesn't have the names of all the places where Jesus has been, Paul. That's not what it's about. When we meet anyone who's not interested in Him, or who won't believe who He is, we mustn't let it make us feel sad or disappointed. We have to remember Josie's arrows. That's the thing that should make us feel better – knowing how far God's message is going to spread. And we *know* it's going to spread!'

Danny nods. He picks up the stick. He drags it through the dust and draws another arrow.

This arrow is long. Very long. It wiggles in and out of Josie's arrows. It stretches all around Paul's map.

And Danny keeps on drawing, walking along, pulling the stick.

Until the arrow stretches right away from the map, all along the dirt track that leads away from Nazareth.

# CHAPTER 15
## No Ordinary Instructions
### (Mark 6:6–12)

Jesus doesn't stay long in Nazareth.

He travels to the villages nearby. There He is able to teach. There the people welcome Him; listen to Him.

They get excited about the message He brings from God: that if they turn to God and ask Him to forgive their sins, then they can be friends with Him. A friendship that will last forever.

'Do you think it's possible,' asks Paul, 'for your feet to wear out if you walk on them too much?'

'Not sure,' says Dave. 'Could be.'

'That's not comforting,' Paul moans. He sits down at the side of the road and slips off a shoe to peer at a large blister on the sole of one foot.

'Think about it,' says Dave. 'If you use anything enough – or more than enough – then in the end you're bound to wear it out. After all, shoes wear out, don't they?'

'And clothes,' adds Benny. 'One minute there isn't a hole. The next, you can't find a patch big enough.'

Paul looks alarmed. 'Really?' He drops his foot to inspect the clothes he's wearing. 'If I had any holes, you'd tell me, right?'

'Of course we would,' grins Benny. 'And don't worry, you haven't. I'm just saying that Dave's right. Stuff wears out.'

Paul nods. 'Good. Great. So, do you think there might be any way to slow Jesus down a bit? Maybe make a few less journeys? Because at the rate He's going, I'm not going to have any feet left.'

Josie chuckles. 'Your feet aren't going to wear out, Paul.'

'Feels like they're worn out already.'

'They're having you on. Your feet are designed to last a lifetime.'

'Are they?' Paul looks at them again and wiggles his toes.

'Well, you've got to take care of them obviously,' says Sarah. 'Nothing lasts if you don't take care of it. But as long as you look after them, they should still be going strong when you're really, *really* old.'

Paul raises his eyebrows. 'Really, *really* old?'

'Really, really, *really* old,' Sarah nods.

'That's good to know.' Paul puts his shoe back on. 'Honestly, though? When you decide to keep up with Jesus here, you have to walk a lot. Really a lot. So lifetime feet come in very handy.'

'Don't you mean feety?' Benny giggles.

Paul gives him a sideways glance.

At last, he gets back up onto his lifetime feet.

'All right,' he says. 'I'm ready.'

Topz walk on. Paul hobbles on his blister.

They've lost sight of Jesus and His disciples but they know there's a village somewhere ahead of them. They're sure that's where Jesus is making for.

Before they reach the village, they find Him.

There He is. His disciples are grouped around Him. He talks to them and they listen without a word. Their faces glow, their eyes sparkle; a mix of fear and excitement.

This isn't an ordinary chat.

These aren't ordinary instructions.

Jesus says, 'I am sending you out, two by two. I am giving you God's authority to help you to spread His message.'

Topz stare. Each one thinks of the arrows in the dust. Josie's arrows.

It's happening right in front of them. God's message is about to spread further. It's about to spread faster.

Jesus tells His disciples, 'When you go, you mustn't take anything with you. Just a stick to lean on and help you with all the walking.'

Paul's eyes light up. 'That's what I need!' he whispers. 'A stick! Then my feet might last even *more* than a lifetime!'

'Take no bread,' Jesus continues. 'Don't take a beggar's bag – you are not to beg in the streets,' He adds. 'And take no money in your pockets. You can wear sandals, but don't take a spare shirt with you.'

Benny frowns. 'What will they do, then?' he murmurs. 'If they can't take anything with them

– no money, no clothes, no food, nothing – how are they supposed to live?'

'I think,' says Dave, 'Jesus is telling them to live by faith. He wants them to trust God. God knows what they need, but Jesus wants them to trust God to provide it all for them.'

**'WOW!'** nods Benny. 'Sounds tough. I mean, I trust God, I do. But to trust Him to give me food when I actually don't have any at all – that's BIG faith.'

'I *want* BIG faith,' says Dave. 'Faith to live like that. I'm going to ask God for BIG faith.'

Benny looks at him and smiles. 'Yeah,' he says. 'Me, too.'

Jesus hasn't quite finished.

'When you go to a place where the people welcome you,' He says, 'stay in the same house there until it's time to leave. And if you arrive in a town where no one gives you a welcome?' He adds. 'Where no one wants to listen to you? Then you are to leave that town. Just shake the dust off your feet and move on. That will be a warning to the people who have ignored you that they shouldn't ignore God.'

The disciples do as they're told.

They obey Jesus' instructions.

Two by two, they visit towns and villages. More towns and villages than Jesus would ever be able to get to on His own.

They teach God's message. They tell people that it's time to change the way they live. It's time to stop doing the wrong things that make God sad; that get in the way of their friendship with Him.

It's time to turn to God.

And Jesus' disciples find that God has given them the power to heal sick people, too. They rub them with olive oil and they make them better.

And so God's message is spread.

Josie's arrows – the ones she scratched in the dirt with a broken, dried-up stick – they are real and alive.

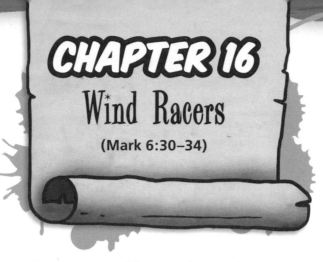

# CHAPTER 16
## Wind Racers
### (Mark 6:30–34)

'Do you fancy a game of hopscotch, Isaac?'

Josie stands next to the grid of numbered squares she's marked out on the ground.

'Isaac, don't do it,' hisses Paul. 'The thing about Josie and hopscotch is you can't win. She's just too good.'

Isaac, the boy from Capernaum, grins at him. 'I like hopscotch. I don't mind giving it a go.'

Paul raises his eyebrows. 'Brave. Definitely brave.'

'We could have a tournament,' says Sarah. 'There are eight of us with Isaac, so we could have four teams of two. We just need to draw some more grids. What d'you think?'

Saucy lies in the sunshine, soaking up the warmth under a brilliant-blue sky. She stretches, opens her mouth wide to yawn.

Paul glances at her. 'I think I'm with Saucy,' he says. **'YAWN ...'**

'Oh, come on,' Sarah answers.

**'YEAH, COME ON, PAUL,'** says Benny. 'We'll be a team. You and me. We'll beat the others, we'll be hopscotch champions. Even Topzscotch champions!'

Paul still doesn't look happy. 'Topzscotch champions. Clever, Benny. Just one thing, though. Do you even know *how* to hopscotch?'

'Do I know how to hopscotch? Don't I look as though I know how to hopscotch?'

'I dunno,' Paul shrugs. 'What does a hopscotcher look like? I mean, you don't look like Josie, and she's the only proper hopscotcher I know.'

'Tch!' Sarah tuts. 'That's nice, isn't it? I'm proper, too.'

'No, I didn't mean ...'

Gruff interrupts; he gets to his feet all of a sudden. Topz' eyes flick towards him. Isaac's, too.

They see the dog's nose twitch as he sniffs the air; hear his little whine. The expectant whine he makes just before he knows John's about to come back, having been off somewhere without him.

Only, John is here. About to play in a Topzscotch tournament.

So who is it Gruff's expecting?

His tail wags. Once or twice; then starts to beat the air furiously.

And just along the road, they see Jesus.

### 'JESUS! JESUS, WAIT!'

Peter's voice. He runs. With James and John and the other disciples, he runs.

Jesus turns and waits for them to catch up with Him. He thinks they are on their own, but then He sees.

Behind them come the people. People who have watched these ordinary men do quite extraordinary things. Who have heard about Jesus and seen what He can do.

Who haven't heard and seen nearly enough, and long for more.

'There's so much to tell You,' Peter says. His voice simmers with excitement. 'We did as You told us to, Jesus. We've been from town to town and village to village. We've met so many people. We've talked to them, we've taught them. We've even been able to heal them!'

Peter's eyes shine. He is tired. All the disciples are tired from the journeys they've made, from all the work they have done.

But still his eyes shine with excitement.

Jesus sees the crowds move along the road in the distance behind them. Move towards them.

'Let's go,' He says. 'You can tell me all your news as we walk, but we should go now. We'll find somewhere quiet. Away from everyone. When we're on our own, you can have a rest.'

They make their way to the lake, slip off in a boat to find somewhere lonely where they can relax together. Out of reach of all the eyes and ears that follow after them. Just for a little while.

But many eyes see them leave. They see the direction of the boat as it sails out onto the lake. They see where it is headed.

They start to bustle and to hurry – to make their way across land to the place where they're sure the boat will come in.

The Topzscotchers go with them, leaving the scratched-out grid behind. Their tournament can wait for another day.

'Shame,' says Paul. 'I was just beginning to like the idea.'

'No, you weren't,' Josie replies.

The people begin to run. Topz, too. How long will it take? Suppose they're not quick enough? If they lose Jesus now, who knows when He will come back to talk to them again? How long will they have to wait?

So they run faster – faster.

They reach Jesus' landing point just before He does.

Isaac laughs. 'That must make us faster than the wind,' he chuckles. 'We beat a sailing boat! We raced the wind.'

The boat at last nudges the shore. Jesus climbs out; He is only half-surprised to discover that the lonely place He thinks He's found isn't lonely at all. It heaves with people.

The disciples step onto the shore with Him and tie up the boat. They look towards Him and wonder what He'll do. Will He be angry that people won't leave Him alone – won't leave *them* alone? He wanted them to have some quiet time together to talk and to rest. That won't happen now.

Jesus casts His eyes over the crowd. He gazes at the hungry faces; hungry for everything that He can teach them; hungry for God. They look so empty. **EMPTY AND IN NEED OF HIM.**

He doesn't feel angry at all. Not even a tiny bit.

He just feels sad for them because they seem so lost.

And almost at once, He begins to teach them.

# CHAPTER 17
## Under Control
**(Mark 6:35–43)**

The day slips past. Until the sun hangs low over the horizon. As it sinks down, the sky is washed in crimson red.

Still Jesus teaches. And the listeners at the water's edge, who stand and lie and sit and sprawl, drink in every word.

They don't care how late it is. They just want to hear more.

'Jesus,' His disciples say to Him. 'Jesus, it's getting so late. The sun has almost set. This is a very out of the way place and everyone must be hungry. Don't You think You should send them away? There must be farms and villages somewhere around here. If they go now, they should still be able to buy themselves something to eat.'

Benny leans towards the other Topz. 'That's a good point. I *am* pretty hungry,' he whispers. 'And it's a long walk back with no food.'

'I didn't bring any bread today,' says Isaac. 'Otherwise we could all share that.'

'Thanks,' Benny says. 'For sharing it if you'd brought any.'

'Well, *my* stomach's grumbling,' whispers Dave. 'Let's hope there's a farm that's close.'

They scramble to their feet. Then they hear Jesus speak again. He looks at His disciples and says simply: '*You* give them some food.'

Jesus' friends glance at each other. Have they heard Him right? They're sure they have. They just don't understand. Food? For all these people? There must be thousands of them! How does Jesus expect them to find something to eat for so many?

'Erm ...' one of them begins. 'Do You want us to go and buy bread for everyone here? I mean, that's going to cost a whole heap of silver coins. Maybe even several heaps.'

Jesus' eyes narrow slightly as He thinks.

'How much bread is there here?' He asks. 'Some people might have brought some with them. Go and find out.'

Isaac clicks his tongue. 'I almost always take bread with me. Almost always,' he mutters. 'I was just in a hurry to get out. And I didn't think I'd be gone nearly all day. Which is silly, because if I see Jesus, I'm always out longer than I think I'll be.'

'It doesn't matter,' smiles Danny. 'We'll be able to get some food from somewhere.'

'No, that's not what I mean,' says Isaac. 'If I'd brought bread with me today, I could have given it to Jesus! To *Jesus*! Then I could have gone home to Mum and said,

"You'll never guess who ate your bread today!" And I'd be right. She would *never guess*!'

The disciples move through the crowd: 'We're going to try to find you some food. Has anyone brought anything with them? If you have and you don't mind, maybe you could give it to us? Then, when we've put it all together, there might be enough to share ...'

Over and over again. They ask the same thing over and over again.

And people shake their heads: 'If we had any food, of course you could have it ... We'd share, only we didn't bring anything ... I was in such a hurry to get after Jesus, I never thought about food. I'm hungry now, mind ... Me, too – but I'm so sorry, I've got nothing ...'

One of Jesus' friends passes close to Isaac and asks the same question. Isaac gives a sad shrug.

'No,' he says. 'I'm sorry.'

It's a while later before the disciples make their way back to Jesus.

They look disappointed. They are tired and hungry themselves.

'This is all there is,' they tell Him. 'Five loaves of bread and two fish. It'll go nowhere, and these people are starving.'

'Tell them all to get into groups,' Jesus says, 'and to sit down on the grass.'

Again the disciples step out into the crowd. They walk in amongst the huddles with Jesus' instructions.

Soon rows of people sit on the ground together. Groups of a hundred. Groups of fifty.

Benny watches Jesus' friends. 'They know there's not enough for everyone,' he murmurs. 'I wonder what they think'll happen. What can Jesus do with a tiny bit of food like that when there are so many people here?'

Dave shakes his head. 'Whatever it is, Jesus will have it all under control.'

'You think?' whispers Isaac.

Dave smiles. 'Jesus has always got it all under control.'

In front of the crowds, Jesus looks up at the sky – up towards heaven. He thanks God for the food He has given them. For the bread and the fish.

He takes the loaves in His hands, breaks them into pieces and passes them to His disciples to share out among the waiting people.

He does the same thing with the two fish; breaks them up so that they can be shared out, too.

And no matter how much bread the disciples give out, there is always a piece left for the next person.

No matter how much fish they share around, the next group of picnickers still have plenty.

The people eat hungrily. They don't understand what has happened. They gaze around astonished, but they eat.

Dave's stomach still grumbles. But he almost can't eat at all.

'This is miracle food,' he murmurs. 'There was almost nothing, but everyone's eating. Everyone's got something. Jesus has made it enough.'

Jesus had made it *more* than enough.

When the disciples go round later to collect up the leftovers, they fill twelve baskets.

# CHAPTER 18
## The Footprint Game

'Guess what?' Benny lies on his back on the beach. Hands behind his head, he gazes up at the moon.

'Don't tell me,' says Sarah. 'You're hungry.'

'No, I'm not actually,' answers Benny. He sounds almost surprised. 'That's miracle food for you. It's a real filler.'

Dave grins. 'If it's filled *you* up, that really *is* a miracle!'

Topz camp on the beach.

After their bread and fish supper, they'd made the long journey back to the far side of the lake. It was almost dark when they left, but the Gang knew they wouldn't get lost. They'd followed hundreds and hundreds of other people, who walked the same bumpy tracks and dusty paths.

As the stars began to twinkle, the moon came up. Round and full; yellow when it first rose, then turning silver against the black-blue of the sky. Its gleam lit the way.

Now Topz lie on the beach out under the stars; out under the moon. Isaac camps with them.

'So, guess again,' says Benny.

'Mmm … no, give up,' answers John.

'Me, too,' says Sarah. 'If you're not hungry, I've no idea.'

Benny springs to his feet. 'I CAN'T SLEEP!'

'I'm so glad 'cos neither can I,' says Josie.

Danny sits up. 'Nor me.'

'Nor me,' says Isaac. He props himself onto one elbow, looking out towards the lake. The surface of the water sparkles in the moonlight, as if it's been scattered with diamonds.

Paul rolls onto his side; hugs his knees in to his chest. He yawns. 'I am actually quite sleepy.'

'Nah!' says Benny. 'You're not sleepy at all. You couldn't be. Not after seeing Jesus do a miracle like that. Five loaves and two fish to feed something like *five thousand* people? No one could be sleepy after that.'

'I wasn't,' answers Paul. 'Not right after. But we've had a really long walk since then. *Really* long.'

'Let's do something,' says Josie. Her eyes reflect the moon. Her voice is eager.

'Well, I'm not doing Topzscotch, so don't even ask me,' grunts Paul.

'Doesn't have to be Topzscotch,' Josie chuckles. 'What else?'

Gruff is up. If John's awake, he's always awake, too. He sniffs in the sand; trots away to sniff more, trots back again and circles John's feet as he stands looking out at the water.

John catches sight of his paw prints. Even in the half-light, they look sharp and clear in the softer sand that stretches away from the lake edge.

**'I KNOW!'** he cries suddenly. **'WE COULD PLAY A FOOTPRINT GAME.'**

Sarah frowns. 'What's a footprint game?'

John jumps up and down. His feet sink into the sand. He points to the marks he's made with both hands.

'We make footprints,' he says. 'But only one of us at a time. Everyone else has to have their eyes closed while they do it so we can't see who's making which prints. Then, when everyone's finished, we have to try to guess whose footprints are whose.'

Sarah looks at John; blinks at him.

Paul sits up on his makeshift bed on the beach. 'D'you know what? That is actually faintly brilliant,' he says.

Benny raises his eyebrows. 'Miracle food is obviously brain food. Stonking idea. So, what are we waiting for?'

'I love that word,' giggles Isaac. '"Stonking" …'

Topz and Isaac find a smooth area of sand a little away from their campsite. One by one, they make their footmarks with their bare feet. Their prints crisscross this way and that way. Some deeper, some more shallow.

Gruff and Saucy make their paw marks there, too. Until the patch of beach is ruffled and pitted and patterned; a jumble of heel and toe marks and claws and pads.

'Now,' says John. They all stare down at the lumpy ground. 'All we have to do is work out whose is whose.'

Still they stare.

'Mmm …' murmurs Benny. 'This could be tricky.'

'Tricky?' says Sarah. 'I'm not even sure which footprints are *mine* anymore, let alone which ones are yours.'

Paul tilts his head to one side, then the other.

'I think,' he says, 'that could be one of yours, Danny.'

Danny squints down to where Paul points. 'Really?'

'Put your foot in it and see,' says Josie.

Danny eases one foot into the foot-shaped dip in the sand. It fits.

'Huh!' beams Paul. 'Good guess.'

Isaac studies the muddle of prints. 'Erm … maybe not,' he says.

He stretches out his leg and places his own foot in the same print. It also fits perfectly.

It's the same with the one next to it. And the one next to that. Danny's feet seem to fit into just about all the prints, too.

The only ones that are obviously different are Gruff and Saucy's.

'I think the trouble is,' says Isaac, 'we've all got just about the same sized feet.'

John's face falls. 'Oh … not such a stonking idea after all, then.'

'But it is!' Isaac's face beams. 'It *is*!'

He throws his head back, stretches both arms upwards and points to the sky.

'Look at the stars! Look at them!'

Topz lift their heads, too; eyes scan the blue-blackness that arches above them, peppered with starlight.

'We don't know how many stars there are, do we? We'll never know,' Isaac says. 'But God knows. Because He put them there.'

He drops his gaze and once again studies the footprints. The jumble, the tangle, the mess of footprints.

'No one could pick out whose feet are whose,' he says. 'No one in the whole world. But God can. Jesus has taught me that. God knows exactly. Because God loves us.'

Topz stare in silence at the prints, back up to the stars, then again at their prints.

'That's why this is such a stonking game, John,' Isaac smiles. 'It shows us how special God thinks we are. He made us, didn't He? Every living, life-full part of us.'

Once again, Isaac stretches his arms upwards, spreads his fingers and lifts his head.

He looks as though he's trying to touch heaven.

'God knows us so well,' he murmurs. 'He even recognises our footprints.'

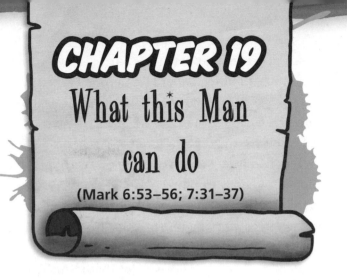

# CHAPTER 19
## What this Man can do
### (Mark 6:53–56; 7:31–37)

Jesus spreads the message of God's love wherever He travels.

With each journey, more and more people hear and are made well. More and more ask for God's forgiveness so that they can have a real friendship with Him. They can live with Him right beside them. Helping them, holding onto them. Forever.

More and more people understand.

Just like Isaac now understands.

Jesus' journeys don't stop. He and His disciples sail again across the lake. The water laps at the wooden boat hull. The breeze is soft; cooling under the sun.

There's a peace out on the water.

A peace that shatters almost the moment they land on the far side at Gennesaret.

They clamber out of the boat, heave on the ropes and tie it up. And instantly people stop to stare.

### 'LOOK!'

They whisper, nudging each other and pointing:

'It's Jesus, I'm sure that's Him … That's definitely Him, I've seen Him before … Why's He here? … Where's He going? … We must let people know. Everyone will want to know! …'

Jesus sets to work again. Together with His disciples, He sets off on foot. Everywhere He goes, people bring ill friends, ill family to Him. People so sick they can only lie on their mats.

In the towns and villages He visits, they crowd into the market places, bringing with them the ones who need healing. They beg Jesus to let them touch just the edge of His cloak.

All who touch it – just brush against it – are made well.

And Jesus teaches them: this is God's power they can see. God's love.

He always reminds them, *this is God.*

Jesus and His friends travel on; close to the city of Tyre, on through Sidon.

When Topz catch up with Him again, it's in a place called Ten Towns. They wonder how many people He's spoken to since they last saw Him; how many people have turned to God, how many people Jesus has healed. Would anyone know?

They remember what Isaac said by the footprints under the stars: God knows. God knows exactly.

'Let us through. Please, please, let us through.'

Danny and Benny turn their heads. They stand back as best they can amongst the jostling crowds to make a way past for the people who try to press towards Jesus.

They can't see Him, these people who want to reach Him. All they can see is the thick huddles in front of them.

But they know He's there. Somehow they have to find a way through with the man they've brought with them. He needs Jesus, this man. He's deaf and he can hardly talk. So his friends and family must listen and speak for him.

'Follow behind them,' hisses Sarah. 'If we follow behind, it makes their group bigger. And a bigger group's got to make more of a pathway.'

Sarah's idea seems to work.

'Let us through. Please let us through,' the man's friends keep saying as they push forward. With Topz pressing along with them, people do drop back; in ones and twos, just enough to let them all pass.

Until at last they see Jesus. And Jesus sees them.

The Gang stay where they are. The people step forward, bringing the man who can't hear or speak with them.

'At last, Jesus. At last we've found You. Please ...' They push the man towards Him. 'Please touch our friend. Place Your hands on him. That's all You need to do. Then he will be able to hear. He'll be able to speak.'

Jesus gazes at the man. He nods His head and beckons to him to follow. He leads him a little way away from the crowd so that He can be with him on his own.

With a light touch, Jesus places His fingers in the man's **EARS**. Gently, He opens the man's mouth and touches his tongue. He looks upwards. Up towards heaven.

He moans as He concentrates. As He calls on God's power.

Then, 'Open,' He says to the man. 'Open up, now.'

And **THE MIRACLE HAPPENS**.

Suddenly the man can hear!

His eyes grow huge as he stares around him; he gazes at Jesus, at the crowd close by. He'd seen them before, of course he had, but now he can hear them; their murmurs, their whispers: 'What's happening? What's going on? Has Jesus done something?'

He can almost hear them breathe!

And he starts to laugh; starts to click his tongue, and then, yes! To talk!

When he looks back towards Jesus, there's such happiness in his eyes; such thankfulness and such wonder.

Jesus watches the man. He glances over at his friends.

'You mustn't talk about this,' He warns.

His voice is firm. He means what He says. He knows how hard it will be for them to keep quiet. Especially for the man who now speaks and hears. Whose whole life has been changed for good and for the better – with a touch of Jesus' hand.

But still, 'You mustn't speak of this,' He says.

Topz overhear. 'They will, though,' says Dave. 'They always do. Jesus tells everyone He heals to keep quiet, but they can't. It's like the more He tells them not to, the more they do it. Because they can't help it.'

The murmurs in the crowd build. There are cries and gasps. They spread back and back through the people as the news travels.

'Look at what this Man can do!' It's all anyone can talk about. 'He makes a man who can't hear *able* to hear; a man who can't talk *able* to talk!

'Just look at what this Man can do.'

# CHAPTER 20
## Touching Heaven

Paul reaches the top of the hill. He's breathless. The slope is steeper than it looks. He gasps in air; sweat prickles across his forehead as he gazes out over the countryside.

He sees the river far away catch the sunlight; a silver streak that glints and winds its way between its banks.

He sees the lake. Perfectly smooth and blue under a perfectly clear-blue sky.

The trees stand so still they don't look real. Crops of corn in the fields seem frozen. Not a breath of wind crosses the ground below the hill. There's nothing to ruffle the things that grow there.

Up higher where Paul has climbed, the tiniest breeze plays with the curls in his hair; just enough to refresh him after his long walk up.

He looks towards the sky. He remembers Isaac the night of the footprints by the lake. How Isaac stretched his arms up to God because right at that moment God was everything to him.

And Paul does the same.

If anyone had been watching, he'd have felt awkward,

he knows he would. Even if he didn't want to feel that way, he knows he would.

But here, all on his own – just him and God – he can do what he wants to do. What he needs to do.

He can tell God exactly how he feels.

He can reach out, like Isaac, and touch heaven.

*I've seen so much, God. Just lately. There's been* **MIRACLE AFTER MIRACLE***. It takes my breath away. Like walking up this hill – it does, it takes my breath away.*

*YOU take my breath away, God.*

*I'm quite – well – practical, aren't I? I'm a practical sort of person. I like to do things; make things. I like maths and puzzles. I like solving stuff. But then, You'd know that because You made me. And You made me like this.*

*So You know I find it hard, God. Hard to say exactly how I feel. I'm just not so good with the wordy bits. Finding the right words and putting them together in the right way to tell You how FANTASTIC I think You are.*

*Because You are, God. You're SO FANTASTIC! You sent Jesus here to change people's lives, and He is. He's changing everything. He's changing how people think about You. How they see You in their heads, how they look at You. He's changing how they talk to You. With every miracle that Jesus does, He shows us how powerful You are.*

*But it's not just Your power that the miracles show. It's Your love.*

*If You didn't love us so much You wouldn't have sent Jesus to show us. It wouldn't matter to You whether we* know You or not. Whether we're friends with You or not.

Whether we get to spend forever with You or not.

It wouldn't matter to You, God. WE wouldn't matter to You.

But we do. We really do! Because You love us.

This is a great hill, God. I love this hill. Up here I CAN **SHOUT AND SHOUT** AND TELL YOU HOW AMAZING YOU ARE WITH WHATEVER WORDS I CAN THINK OF!

And no one else can hear me, God! No one else can see me! 'Cos just at this moment, the only One I want to hear me and see me is You. Sometimes it needs to be just me and You. And no one else in the whole wide world.

It's like that for Jesus, isn't it? He goes off to be alone with You. It's hard for Him to find places to be on His own, because everyone follows Him. Us Topz do.

But when He does find somewhere – somewhere for just You and Him – that time must be so special.

I get tired, God. And when I'm tired, I get grumpy. Even when Jesus gets tired – and He must get tired because He never stops working for You – He never sends anyone away. He doesn't turn His back on a single person who comes to Him for help. He makes them better. Or He talks to them. The disciples don't always understand what's going on, I can see it in their faces. But Jesus doesn't get cross with them. He doesn't give up on them. He keeps teaching them.

He keeps showing You to them.

I want to be like Jesus, God. I never want to get tired of working for You. Please help me.

And I'm sorry if I don't always know the right words

to tell You how I feel. Sarah's good at that. Dave, too. But I guess You know how I feel anyway.

And right now, God, I just want You to know that I love You. I LOVE YOU!

See my arms, God? See my hands? I'm reaching out to You.

I'm touching heaven.

# CHAPTER 21
## Into the Daylight
(Mark 8:22–26)

'How much bread do you think the average person eats in a lifetime?' Benny asks.

Topz sit on the riverbank in the shadow of a tree. They munch on a bread picnic. Jesus has gone to Bethsaida, a village a little way off. They've stopped trailing after the followers to sit by the river and have something to eat. They'll catch up later.

'Not a clue,' answers Paul. 'I'd have to do a lot of working out to answer that one. I mean, for a start, the average person may not even *like* bread.'

Benny frowns. 'Not like bread? Living here? That'd be tricky, wouldn't it? Bread's really important here.'

Paul shrugs. 'But if you don't like it, you don't like it. Not a lot you can do. And,' he adds, 'some people can be allergic. Don't forget that.'

Benny throws him a sideways glance.

'If I didn't like bread,' says Danny, munching a crust and enjoying every mouthful, 'I think I'd eat it anyway. If there was nothing else, I'd just eat it.'

'Don't know if *I* would,' says Sarah. 'I think I might

have to go and look for some fruit or something.'

'Yeah,' answers Danny, 'but if there wasn't any, you'd have to eat the bread, wouldn't you?'

Sarah shakes her head. 'I'd find some fruit. I know lots of places to look for fruit.'

'Erm, as interesting as this is,' says Benny, '– I mean I love the whole "bread versus nothing versus fruit" argument – but what does it have to do with my original question – how much bread do you think the average person eats in a lifetime?'

'Nothing,' Danny replies. 'We just don't know the answer, so we thought we'd talk about something else.'

'Fair enough ...' Benny nods.

He's quiet for a moment. Then he starts to fidget; then to whistle.

'Shall we play "spot the fish"?' he asks suddenly. His face brightens.

Josie chuckles. 'You're not very good at just sitting, are you, Benny?'

'Well, what's good about just sitting? I've finished my bread. Nothing left to sit *for*. So ... shall we play "spot the fish"?'

Topz lie at the edge of the bank; stretched out, stomachs down, chins propped in hands. They peer downwards. They watch the river run.

The water trickles and flows past their eyes. In ripples and creases, and swirls where it washes into rocks; glitters bright in the sunlight. Below the surface, silky-green waterweed moves with the current, wriggles and waves and dances.

'There!' Josie's up on her knees. She points.

'Where?' Benny follows her finger.

'There, right there!'

Sunshine glints off a coat of scales. The fish flashes silver. It's gone as soon as it's spotted.

'But *where*?' Benny asks again.

The fish was too quick. No one else saw.

'That's one to me, then,' grins Josie.

'Well, not really,' says Benny. 'If no one else saw it, you could have imagined it.'

'Benny, I didn't imagine it. I saw a fish. So that's one to me.'

'Yeah, but it could have been something else.'

'Uh, like what?' Josie demands.

'I dunno,' shrugs Benny. 'Like ... a sandal?'

**'OH, A SANDAL!'** Josie says. **'WHY DIDN'T I THINK OF THAT?** A sandal that just happens to look *exactly* like a fish. **UGH!'**

'It's possible.'

'No – it's not! I saw a fish, Benny, and it actually was *a fish*!'

Dave pushes up onto his knees. 'I think maybe we need some rules.'

'Rules?' Josie frowns. 'You mean like, if you spot a sandal, you must not try to pass it off as a fish?'

Dave grins. 'Not exactly. Just, maybe a fish has to be seen by two of us to actually count as a fish spot.'

'Good idea,' agrees Danny.

'Yup,' nods John.

Josie shakes her head. 'That is *so* not fair.'

'Yeah, but rules are rules,' says Benny. 'Shall we start again, then?'

Just as Josie's about to drop back onto her stomach – 'Wait a minute!' Sarah hisses. 'Look.'

They turn their heads to look where Sarah looks.

In the distance, Jesus walks.

Topz had planned to find Him later in Bethsaida. Now He has found them.

He's not alone. There's a man who walks with Him. Jesus seems to have him by the hand.

Jesus leads him.

Topz watch in silence. Then, 'He's blind,' murmurs Paul. 'That man with Jesus – he's blind.'

As soon as they realise, they understand why Jesus and the man are there.

They know what they are about to see. They don't move; don't speak. They wait.

The man doesn't speak either. He stands in front of Jesus. He can't see Him. Behind his eyes is just darkness.

But he knows exactly who Jesus is. Like Topz, he dares to believe that he knows what is about to happen.

Behind them, far along beside the river, there are people. Jesus has led the man away out of Bethsaida. But the people have followed them.

Jesus looks into the man's face; deep into the eyes that can't see. He closes His own eyes a moment; places His hands on those of the man.

'Now look. Look about you. What can you see?' Jesus asks. His voice is quiet, like the tiniest breath of wind.

Again, Jesus speaks. 'Can you see anything?'

The man turns his head. Just a little. He peers around; half afraid to look at all in case there is just the darkness.

He catches his breath. Is this real? Is it just shadows that move in the blackness behind his eyes?

'I think ... I think, yes ... I think I see people ... People, but they don't exactly look like people. They look like trees that walk along ...'

Once again, Jesus touches the man's eyes; He covers them with His hands.

When He takes them away, this time the man's face is determined. Brave.

This time he *wants* to see. He knows that he *will* see.

In that moment, his eyes clear. They gleam. Brighter than the silver flash of fish scales Josie saw. More brilliant than the glitter of sunlight off the river.

The man screws his eyes up against the glare of daylight.

He gasps in one sharp breath and then another.

He sees the people who walk towards them. He sees their faces. They are still some way off, but he sees every detail of their faces.

He sees the trees along the bank and the tufts of grass underfoot. The blue arch of the sky overhead, the sparkle of the river nearby.

He sees Jesus. And the eyes that gleam fill with tears. Such thankful tears.

'Don't go back to the village,' Jesus says. 'Go home, but don't go back to the village.'

The people of Bethsaida will be full of questions. Too many questions.

Jesus doesn't want news of the miracle to spread. It's still not time.

But the news is too great. Too huge. No one can keep quiet about news like that. So it spreads anyway.

# CHAPTER 22
## Not the End
### (Mark 9:30–32)

John sits by himself on the edge of a field.

The miracle of the blind man still dances in his mind. How he walked towards Topz in darkness but walked away in dazzling daylight. The man's beaming, glowing face; his sparkling, sky-bright eyes – John can't forget them. He doesn't want to forget them.

The man who couldn't see was so determined. When Jesus touched his eyes that second time, he completely believed. He had no doubts.

Jesus would heal him. Jesus *did* heal him.

Words chase around John's head. Words he has heard Jesus speak; that all of Topz have heard Him speak.

*'Everything is possible for the person who has faith.'* (Mark 9:23)

From the stony track behind him, John hears voices. He scrambles to his feet and slips into the field. He crouches down to hide between the rows of corn.

This is still his time. His alone time. He doesn't want to have to share it with anyone else. Not right now.

The voices come closer. Feet crunch over gravel.

There is laughter. These are friends.

It's Peter's voice John recognises first. Then the voice of Jesus.

John stays hidden. Jesus sometimes walks with His disciples away from the towns and villages. Away from the lake. He needs time apart from the crowds, too. Time to be on His own with God; time to teach His disciples. There is so much they need to learn.

John doesn't want to disturb Jesus' alone time any more than he wants his own disturbed. He stays out of sight.

The men fall silent. When Jesus speaks again, His voice is calm; serious.

'We've talked about this before,' He says. 'I, the Son of Man, will be arrested. I will be handed over to the people who hate me. Who don't want to listen to me because they don't like what I have to say.

'These people have their own rules about how to worship God. And because they bury themselves in their rules, they have lost sight of Him.

'These people will kill me.'

John bites his lip. The words are not for him to hear but he can't help hearing them. Jesus speaks them for His disciples' ears. But they turn his heart to ice.

'Listen to me, though!' Jesus says. 'Three days later, I will come back to life. It's not the end. Three days later, *I WILL LIVE AGAIN!*'

There's not a sound.

No one talks or moves. Not a whisper of breeze rustles the corn.

Until once more John hears the crunch of stones under feet. The disciples walk on after Jesus. They don't understand what He's said, but they don't ask Him to explain.

They're afraid. Why does He talk about His death? They're afraid to know what He means.

John is afraid, too.

Alone in the cornfield, he thinks of the blind man who can now see. Because of Jesus he can now see.

He thinks of a world without the **MIRACLE MAKER**. And he's afraid.

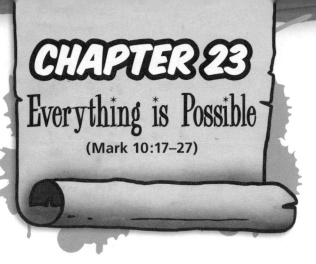

# CHAPTER 23
## Everything is Possible
### (Mark 10:17–27)

The marketplace buzzes.

Sarah holds tight to Saucy. Gruff trots at John's heels.

'You should let Saucy walk more,' says Benny.

'I can't, not here,' answers Sarah. 'Way too many people. She'd get lost, you know what she's like.'

Benny nods towards Gruff. 'Gruff's being pretty good,' he says. 'Can't you train her to be like Gruff – and just sort of follow?'

Sarah gives him a withering look. 'For one thing, Benny,' she says, 'Gruff doesn't always "just sort of follow". He can do exactly the opposite of what you want him to do when he feels like it. For another, Saucy's a cat. You can't train cats the same way as you can dogs. They're too independent. They like to think for themselves. And for *another* thing,' she adds, 'what makes you think Saucy would want to be like Gruff?'

'Come to think of it,' says John, 'what makes you think Gruff would *want* Saucy to be like him?'

Benny shrugs. 'Just a suggestion.'

Topz walk on away from the town. The market was busy, but in the distance it's busier still.

Jesus is teaching. If there are people to listen, He talks to them about God.

Topz have almost reached Him when a man runs past them.

The people up ahead are turning away now; heading back to town. Jesus is about to leave. So the man runs to catch Him.

When he reaches Him – stands in front of Him – he drops to his knees.

'Teacher,' he says. He's out of breath, but he needs to speak. 'Good Teacher, please. You talk about eternal life. You teach about being able to live with God forever. What must I do? Please tell me. What must I do to have this eternal life?'

Jesus stares at him.

'Why do you call me that?' He asks. 'You call me "good" – why? It's only God who is truly good.'

Again He watches the man.

'Tell me,' Jesus says. 'You know the commandments, don't you? You must not murder anyone; you must not commit adultery; you must not steal; you must not tell lies about someone; you must not be a cheat; you must respect your parents.'

The man listens intently. He hears Jesus' words and he looks pleased with himself.

'Yes!' he nods. 'Yes, of course I know these commandments. And I obey them, Teacher. I've obeyed them since I was a child.'

Still Jesus gazes at him.

Benny steps forward and makes his way through the people who walk towards him, who have begun the journey back to their homes.

He finds a place to stand. A place so close to Jesus that he can almost see right into His eyes.

And as Jesus looks at the man who still kneels in front of Him, those eyes are filled with love.

'This is what you must do then,' Jesus says to him. 'To live with God forever, there is only one thing you must do. You must sell everything you have. Sell it all, and give the money you make to poor people who have nothing. If you do that,' Jesus says, 'then there will be many riches for you in heaven. And when you've sold everything,' He adds, 'come and follow me.'

The man's face falls. Just as Jesus knows it will.

Sell *everything*? This man is rich. Very rich. If he sells everything he has and gives the money away, he will lose so much. He will end up with nothing.

How could he be happy to end up with nothing?

It's in the way he hangs his head. It's in his eyes: *I will do many things. I want to do many things to have a life with God. But this, Jesus? Give up everything I have? This is too much.*

The man gets to his feet. He doesn't look pleased with himself anymore. He looks sad. He knows he can never do as Jesus tells him to do.

Jesus knows it, too.

Disappointed, shoulders drooping, the man ambles slowly away.

Benny watches him. Then his eyes flick back towards Jesus. Will Jesus just let him go?

Jesus glances round at His disciples. They have heard every word.

He says to them, 'Do you see how hard it is for rich people to enter God's kingdom?'

The rich man still wanders away. Jesus doesn't call him back; doesn't go after him. If he wants to obey Jesus, if he wants to follow Him – he has to decide to do it for himself.

And he has to decide happily. Willingly.

The disciples look shocked. Is there no other way for this man? Surely there must be another way!

Jesus knows their thoughts.

'It is so hard for some people to give their lives to God,' He says. 'Let me tell you this – it is harder for a rich man to enter God's kingdom than it is for a camel to get through the eye of a needle.'

'Then how,' Jesus' friends cry, '*how* can anyone be saved to be with God forever?'

Jesus looks at them. At each one of them.

He shakes His head. 'It's impossible for you,' He says. 'For *people*, it is impossible. But it's not impossible for God.'

He steps towards them. He looks at them with such love. Benny sees it shining in the deep pools of His eyes.

'For God, you see, everything is possible,' Jesus smiles. 'Never forget. *Everything* is possible for God.'

**'BENNY!'**

Benny hears Dave call his name. 'We're heading back to town, Benny, are you coming?'

Benny lifts a hand and waves vaguely.

He doesn't answer. He doesn't move.

He understands now.

It's God who clears the way for people to be a part of His kingdom.

People need to turn to Him; to give their lives over to Him. But it's God who makes it possible for them to be with Him forever.

Benny breathes in a deep breath; fills his lungs, feels full of the life God has given to him.

'Thank You,' he whispers. 'Thank You for being the *everything's possible* God.'

His eyes drift up to look into the sky.

'For being MY *everything's possible* God.

**THANK YOU** ...'

# Colourful daily Bible reading notes just for you

In each issue the Topz Gang teach you biblical truths through word games, puzzles, riddles, cartoons, competitions, simple prayers and daily Bible readings.

Available as an annual subscription or as single issues.